Color Me Bright

Coloring Book #2

by

Nadja

NadjaMedia.com

NadjaMedia.com

Nadja Media
530 Los Angeles Ave., Suite 115
Moorpark, California 93021

ISBN – 13: 978-1-942057-98-7
ISBN – 10: 1-942057-98-9

No liability is assumed for damages resulting from the use of or misinterpretation of information contained herein. Nadja never advocates the use of violence in any form or for any reason. The designs were created for people to enjoy coloring in and also for creating their own designs within the empty template outlines.

The artist/author of this book is not a medical doctor and does not dispense medical advice, diagnose, or prescribe the use of any technique or object as a form of or substitute of treatment for physical, emotional, or medical problems without the advice of your health care provider, either directly or indirectly. Check with your health care provider before working with these designs to make sure they do not conflict with your health program. If expert assistance or counseling is needed, the services of a competent professional should be sought. The artist/author and publisher assume no responsibility for your actions or interpretations of the designs or words in this book.

Dedication

To Creativity.

May we discover this wonderful gift that was bestowed upon all of us without exception.

May we use it to help heal ourselves, the world, and enter into joy and fulfillment.

Acknowledgments

I want to acknowledge all the artists from antiquity up to the present time for inspiring our creative efforts though their example. The top five living artists who have mentored me are SARK, Shiloh Sophia, Shari McComb, Aviva Gold, and Rassouli.

Foreword

Welcome. Thank you for purchasing this book. It was created for your enjoyment and provides many hours of relaxing interactive entertainment. There are 65 designs waiting for you to bring them to life.

I have been drawing these patterns since fourth grade, but had never thought to color them in until the coloring books for adults phenomena took the book market by storm. Perhaps it is the unrest in our world that is driving us all to seek some kind of relief where we can enjoy ourselves in this way. Coloring keeps us focused on the moment, away from all the hubbub and information overload. This activity has helped many to decompress, unplug, relax, let go, and enjoy creating and completing something of beauty. It is a type of art therapy that helps calm the mind, renew the spirit, and provide creative fulfillment.

Bright colors have been documented to lift our mood, our frequency. I love using neon and fluorescent Laneco gel pens, Gelly Roll pens, and Tombow ABT pens. I also like to use PaperMate Sharpwriter #2 mechanical pencils for outlining patterns or you could use a thin to thick line black pen. Another fabulous tool for correcting errors is the Uni-Ball UM 153 Signo Broad Point Gel Pen, White.

There are 4 tester pages at the end of this book for you to experiment with your coloring tools, colors, shading, and color combinations before you take the plunge to color a page. YouTube.com has many informative tutorials about tools, tips, and techniques to use in coloring books for adults (including shading with water color on top of colored pencil or pens). All coloring pages are printed on one side only to allow for bleeding through of ink or watercolor. It would be wise to put a thick piece of paper like cardstock underneath the page you are coloring for extra bleed through protection. The words on the back of every page were necessary due to layout rules for printing. I selected words that should lift your spirit, make you smile, and put a song in your heart. The numbers on the back of each pattern help identify it.

You can frame the pages you absolutely love. The images work upside down or flip either way sideways as well. Put them up in your house or give them as gifts (always credit this book and author). Have fun, explore, and enjoy using this book. If you are really enthusiastic about it, please tell others and post a review on social media and Amazon. You can also exhibit your best work at Hashtag: #ColorMeBrightCB (CB stands for Coloring Book). When you do this you could post your first name, country or state, book number (1, 1a, 2, 2a – 4 coloring books in this series), and the identifying number on the back of the pattern. (Example: PattyCA2CB56) Also check out my website at NadjaMedia.com as I may have an art contest featuring a specific page.

If you are eager to continue on after you complete this book there is Color Me Bright Coloring Book #1 with 65 more designs to color in. Then for advanced colorists and those who like to bump it up a notch, there are Color Me Bright Coloring Book #1a and Color Me Bright Coloring Book #2a. These contain the empty template outlines that match the designs in the original books page by page. They are meant to be used together so that you can either copy the design into the empty template outline or you can create your own designs within it to color in.

Now, get your colors ready, get cozy, and color yourself into the flow.

— **Nadja**

Reviews

"This coloring book is amazing and clearly channeled. One of those 'transmissions' that comes through beyond the processing of even the author (or conduit) herself! These designs trigger the DNA memory fields through symbol and art. They are memory triggers, yet by coloring these symbols in, you actually take part in their creation (and thus the creation of the memory trigger).

My advice is to follow these absolutely intuitively. Look through them and choose the one that calls to you and spend as little or as much time on the symbol as you need. These can be used for manifestation, balance and awareness and are really practical 'ascension tools' to be used by children and adults alike.

I love them! Nadja has a real gift. I know she is one of many of these individuals that hold 'the Artist's Eye' and are able to bring forward channeled message in the form of symbol bypassing the left brain completely and going straight to the right brained awareness and speaking directly to the heart (and the DNA)."

— Magenta Pixie, Channel for the 'White Winged Collective Consciousness of Nine,' Author of **Masters of the Matrix**: Becoming the Architect of Your Reality and Activating the Original Human Template and **Divine Architecture and the Starseed Template**: Matrix Memory Triggers for Ascension. Visit her at MagentaPixie.com or on YouTube.

****

"What I envision for this particular coloring book is that it may even help autistic children and adults to restore their brain deficits. It could be classified as complementary medicine in the future as we progressively understand more about the science of motor skills, neurochemistry, and pathophysiology as related to autism. Art therapy is a unique form of treatment for autism. It fosters long-term benefits for mitigating symptoms by providing autistic behaviors an expressive, creative outlet. This therapy promotes communication, emotional growth, and sensory integration. It can also encourage social interaction as the art may become a focal point of sharing."

— Sarah Larsen, M.D., Host of Miracle Makers on Universal Broadcasting Network, Founder of Miracle Makers Academy, and Medical Intuitive. Dr. Sarah leads spiritual tours to Egypt, India, and Italy. Her website is DrSarahLarsen.com.

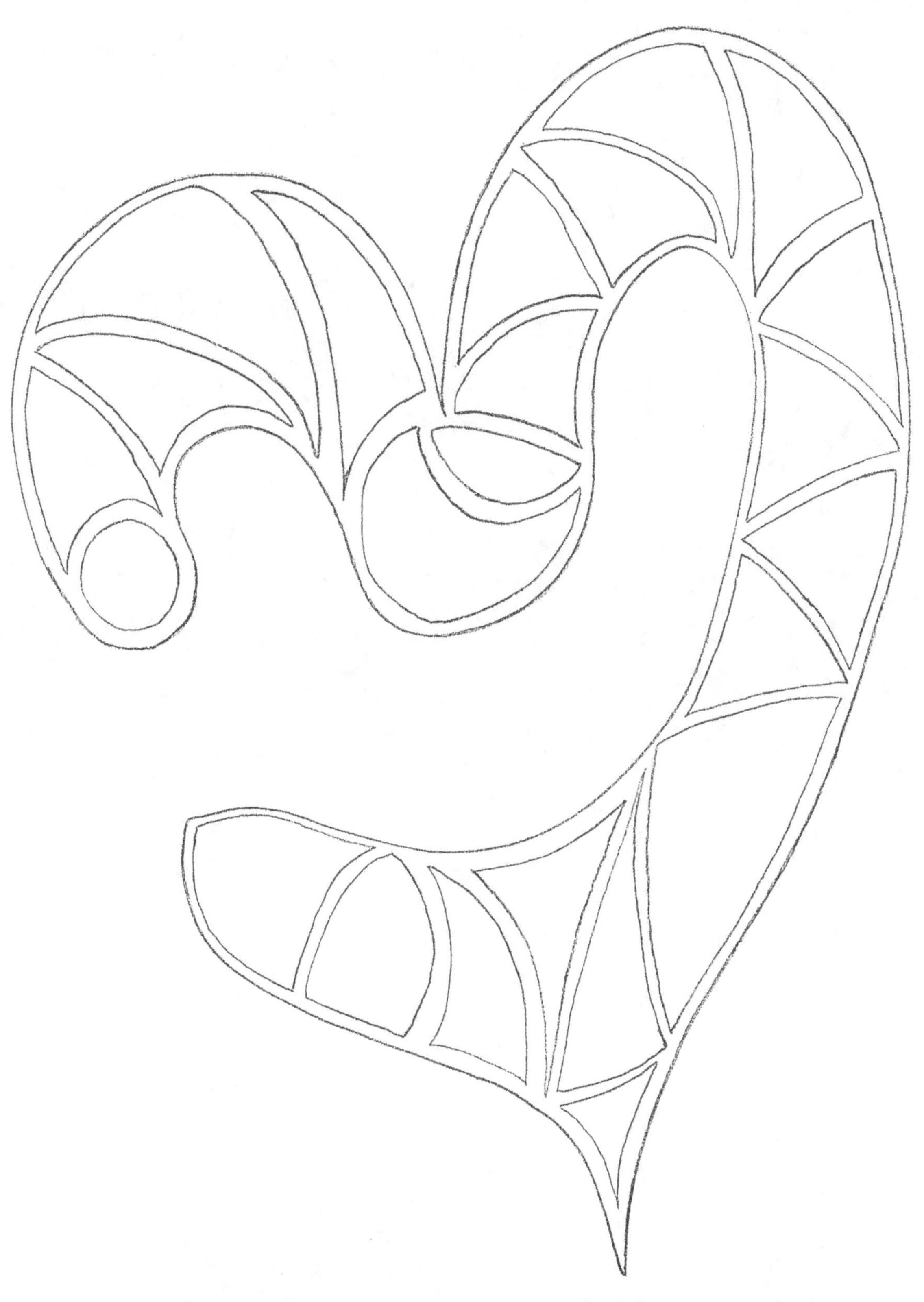

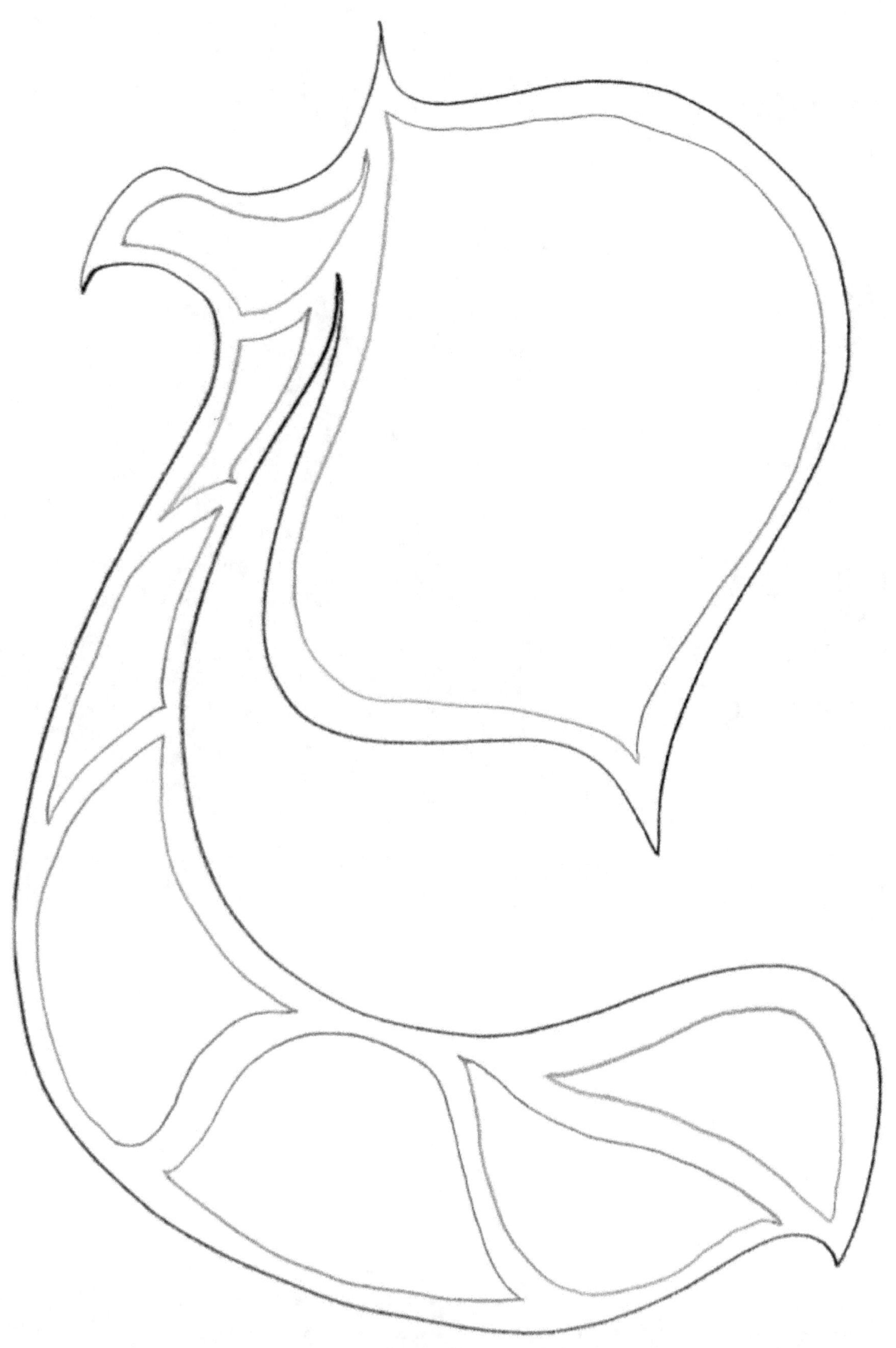

#2Cactus #ColorMeBrightCB

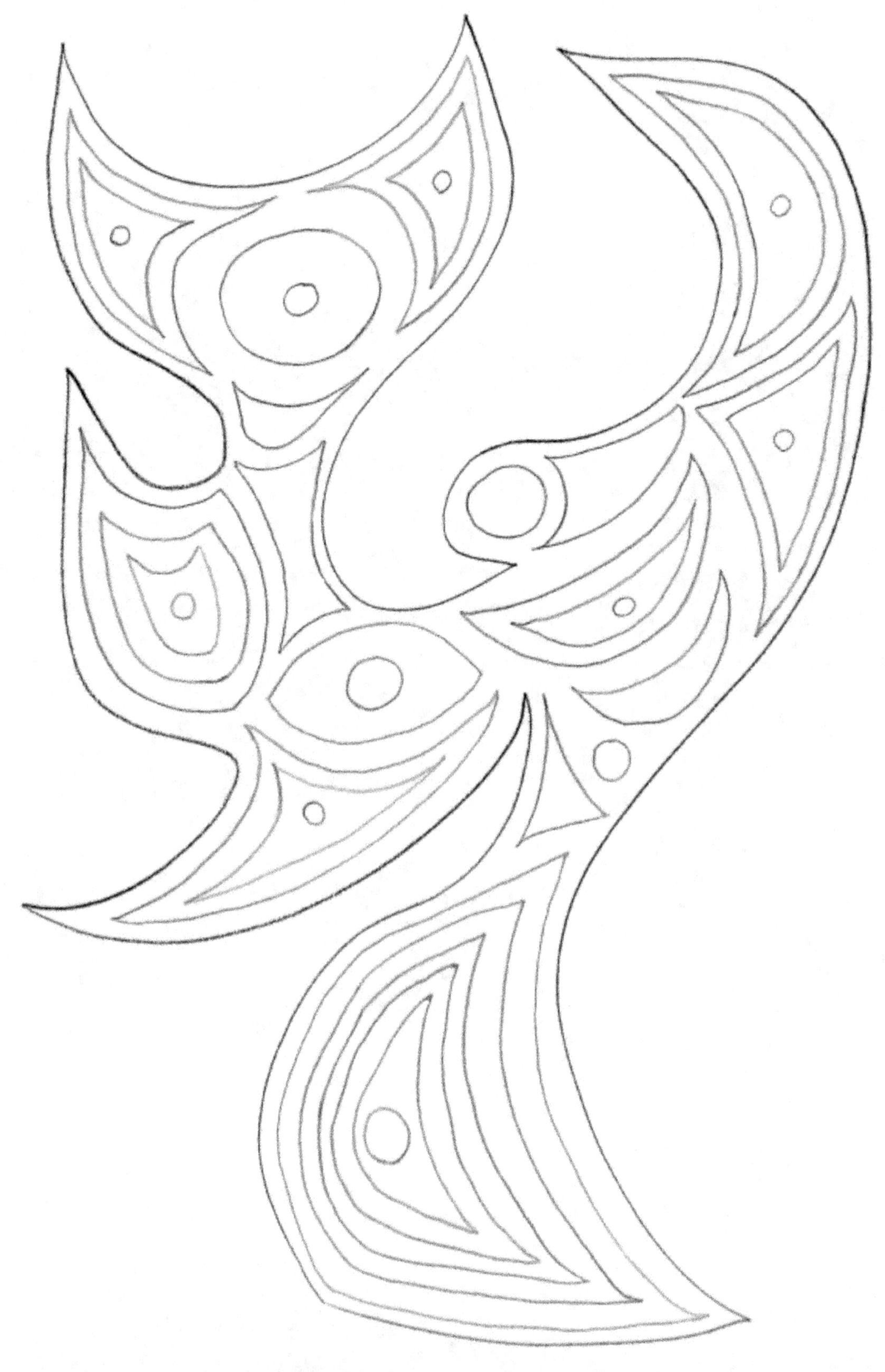

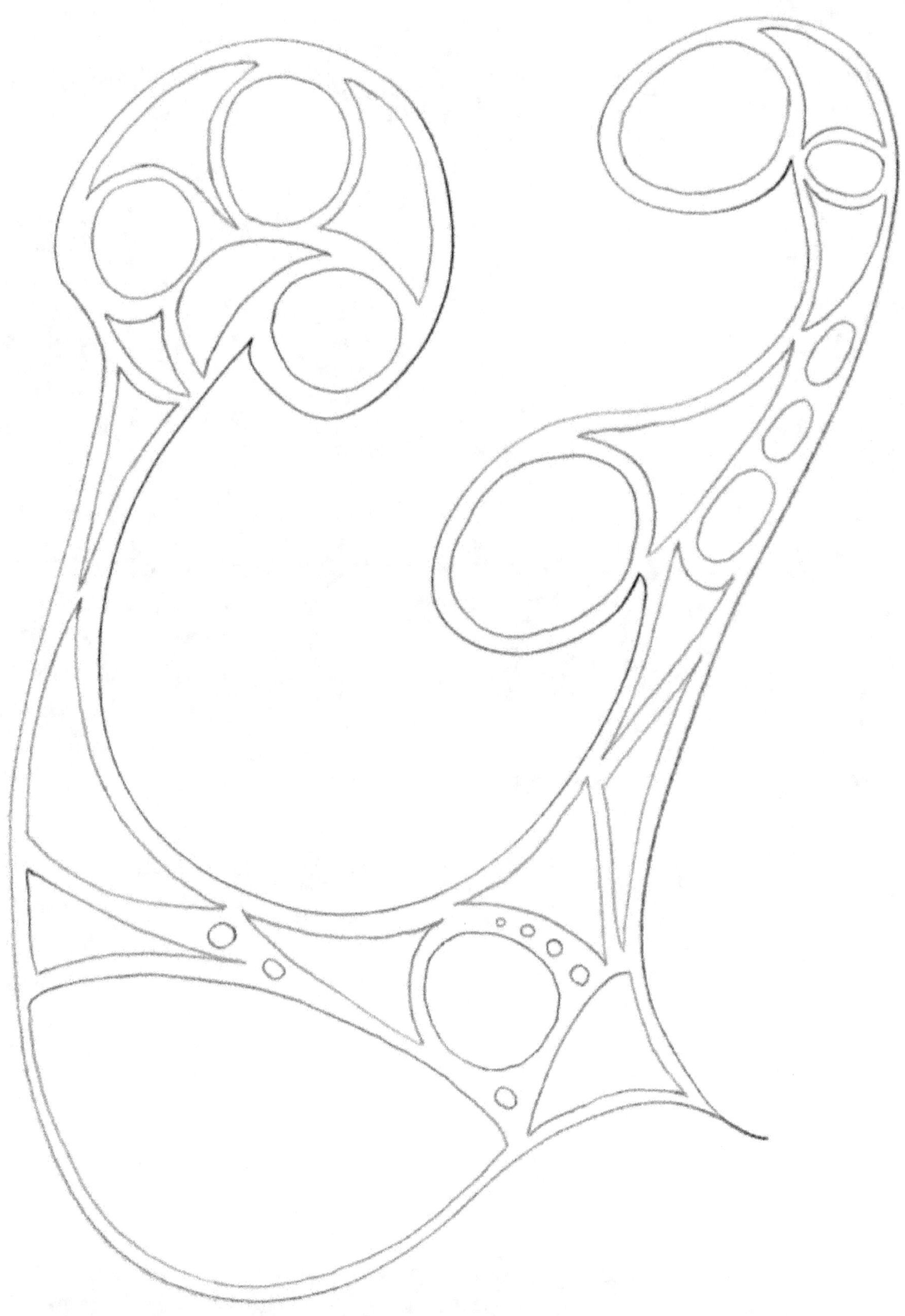

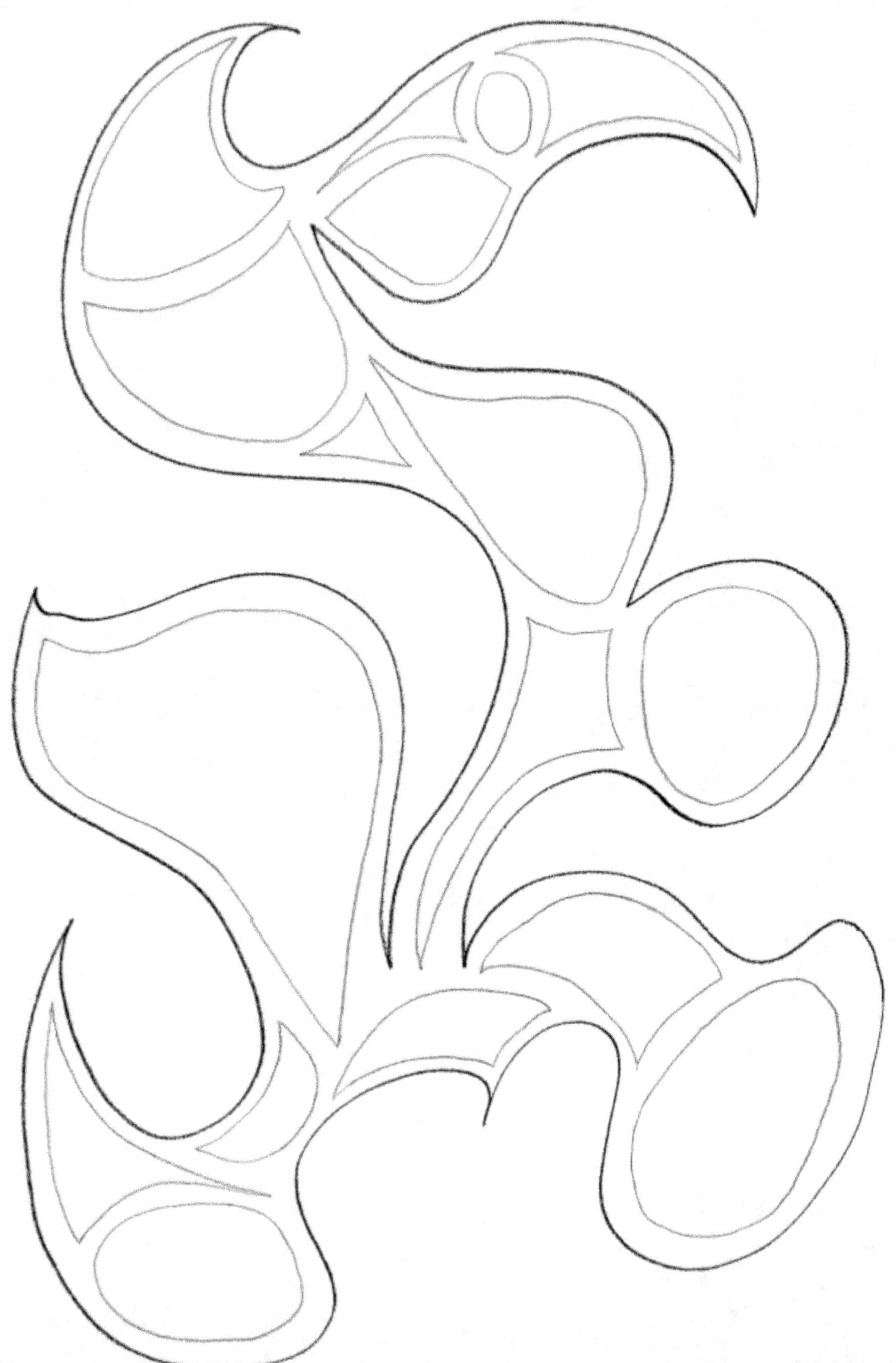

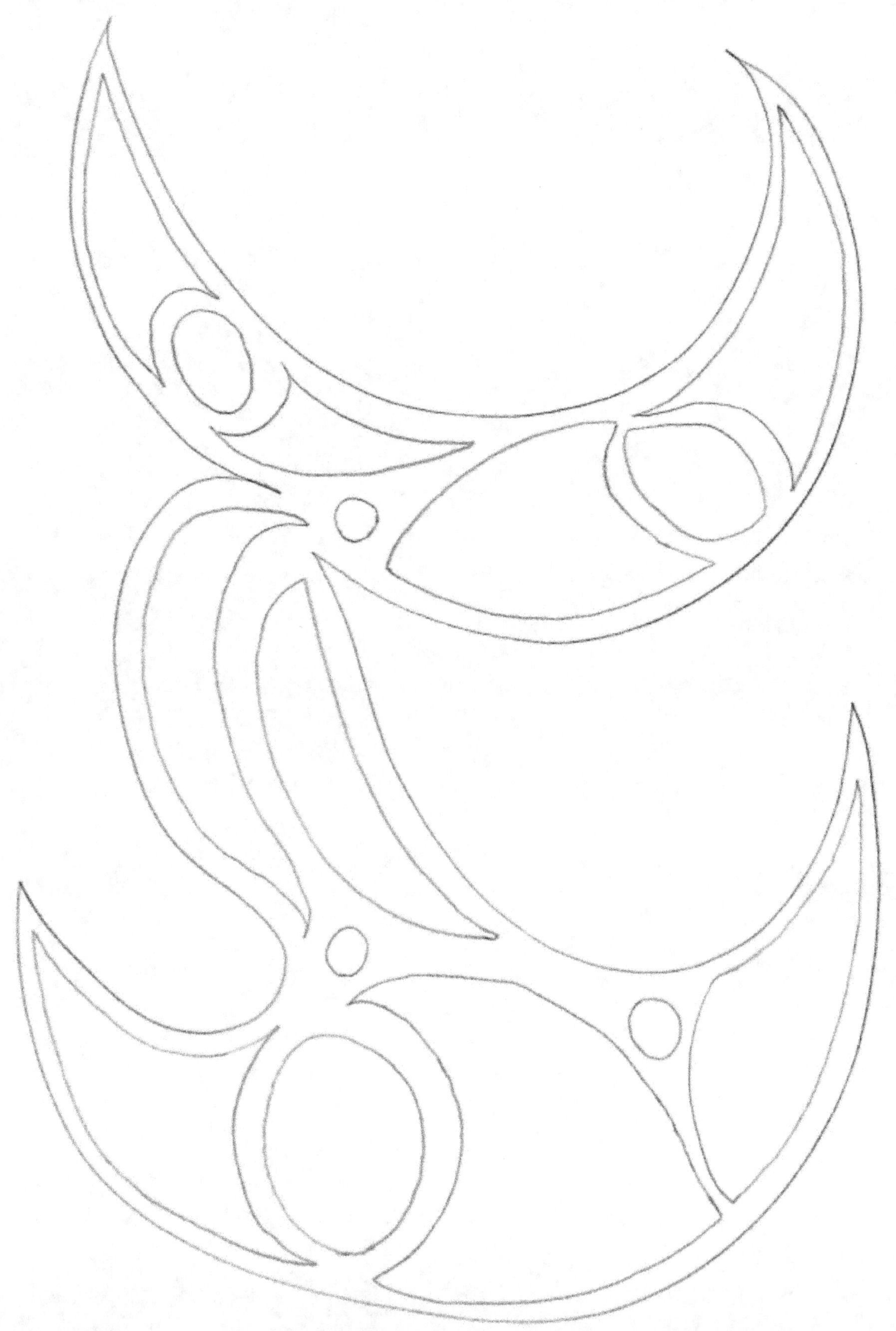

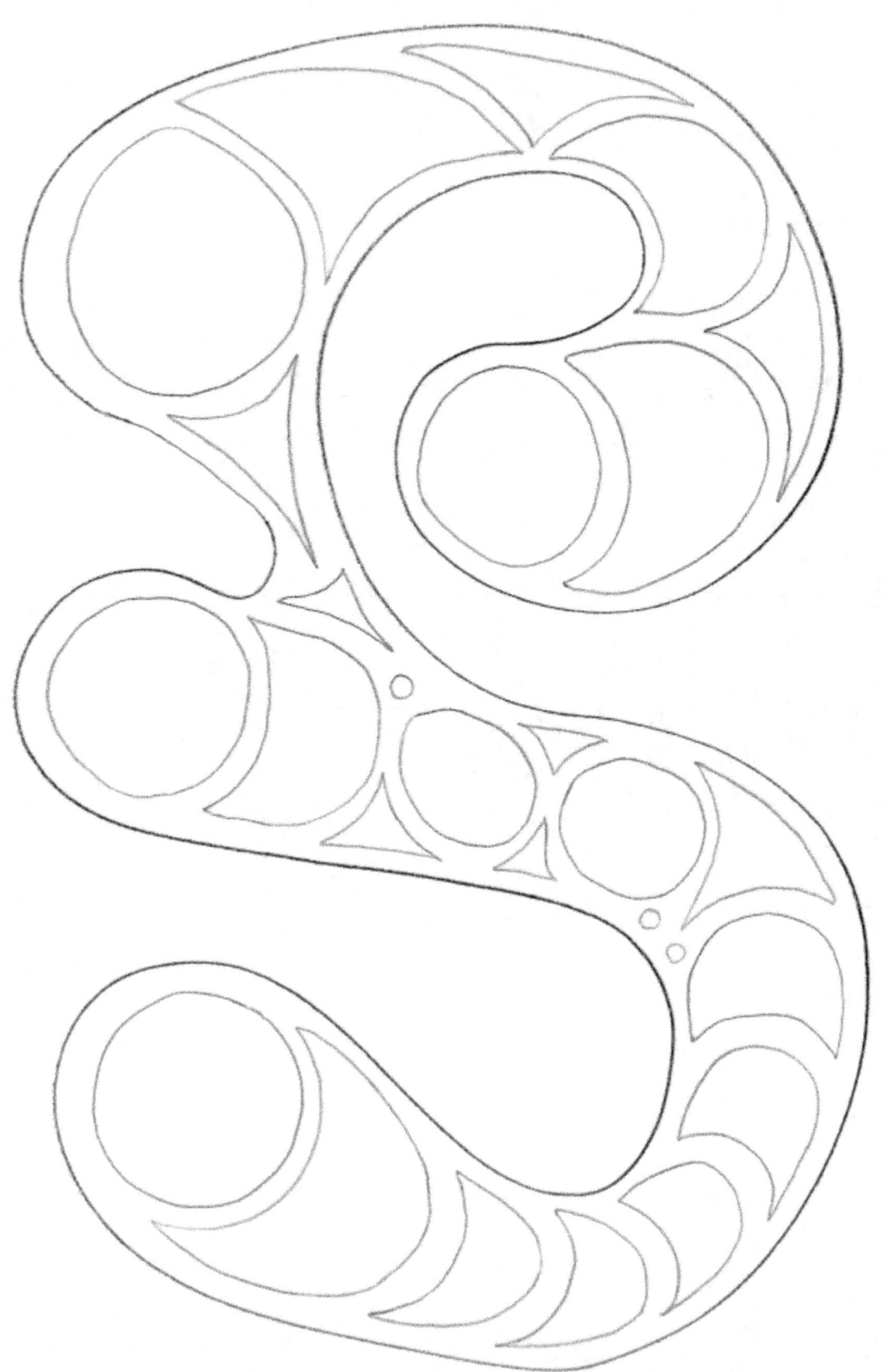

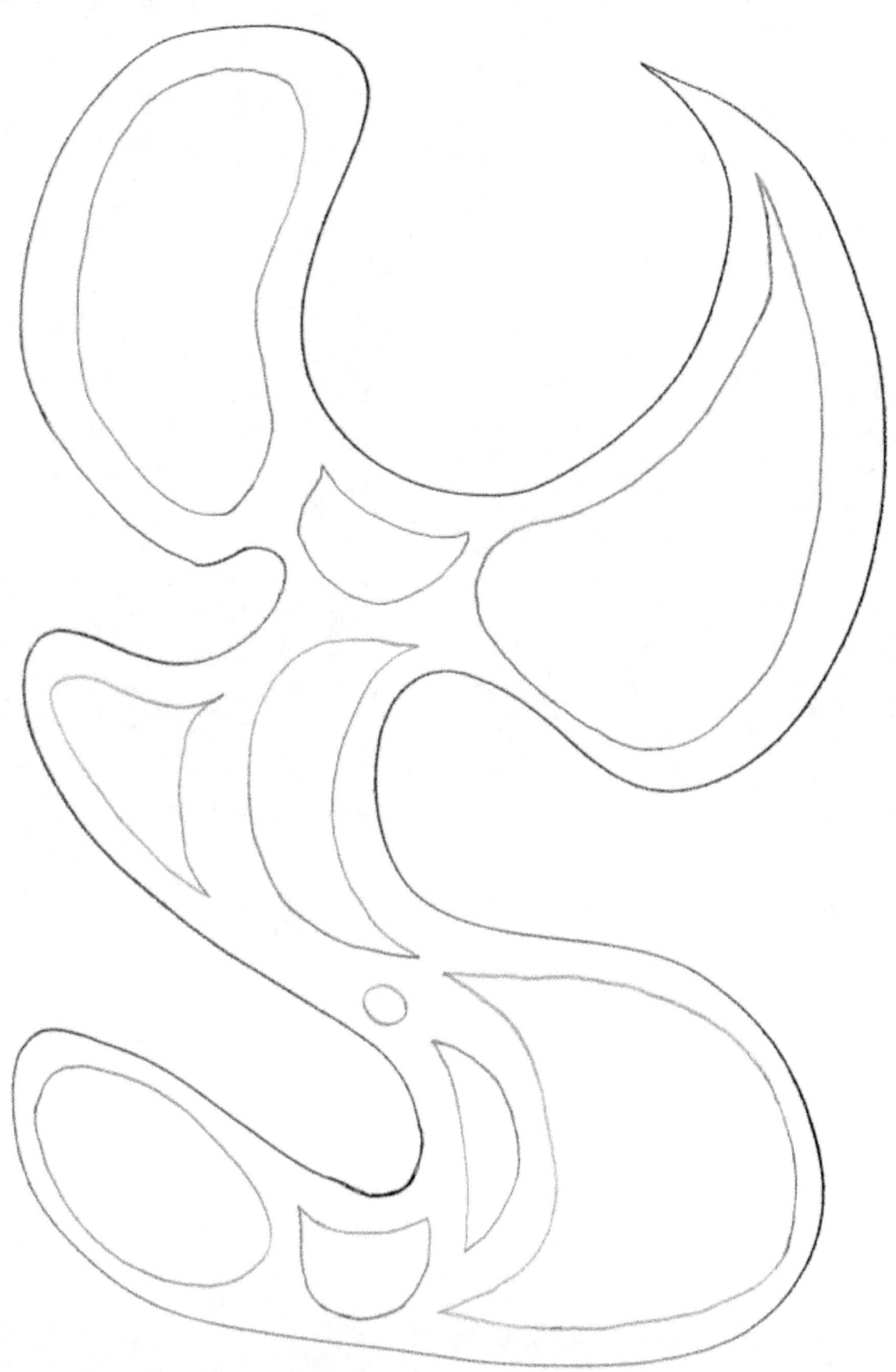

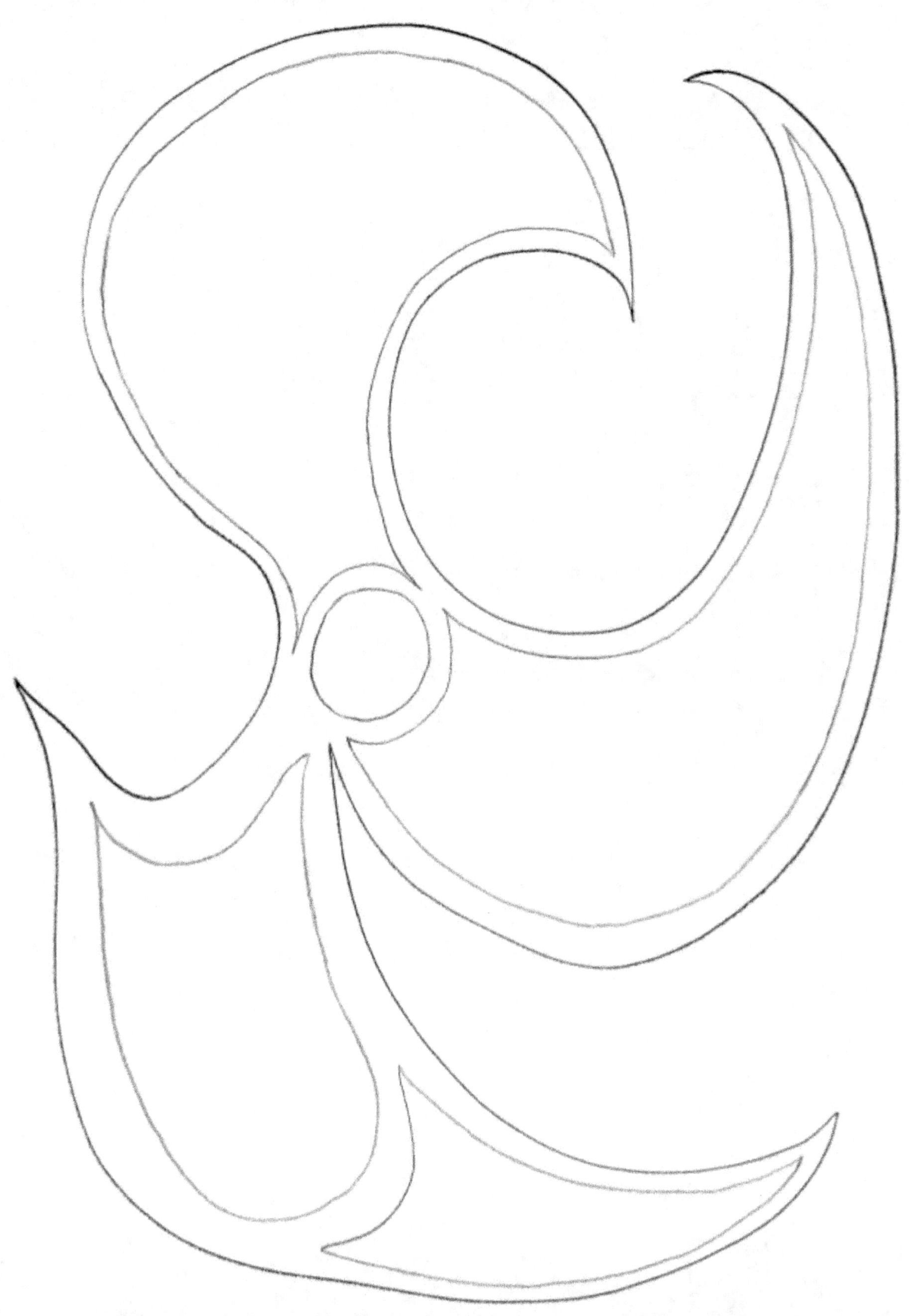

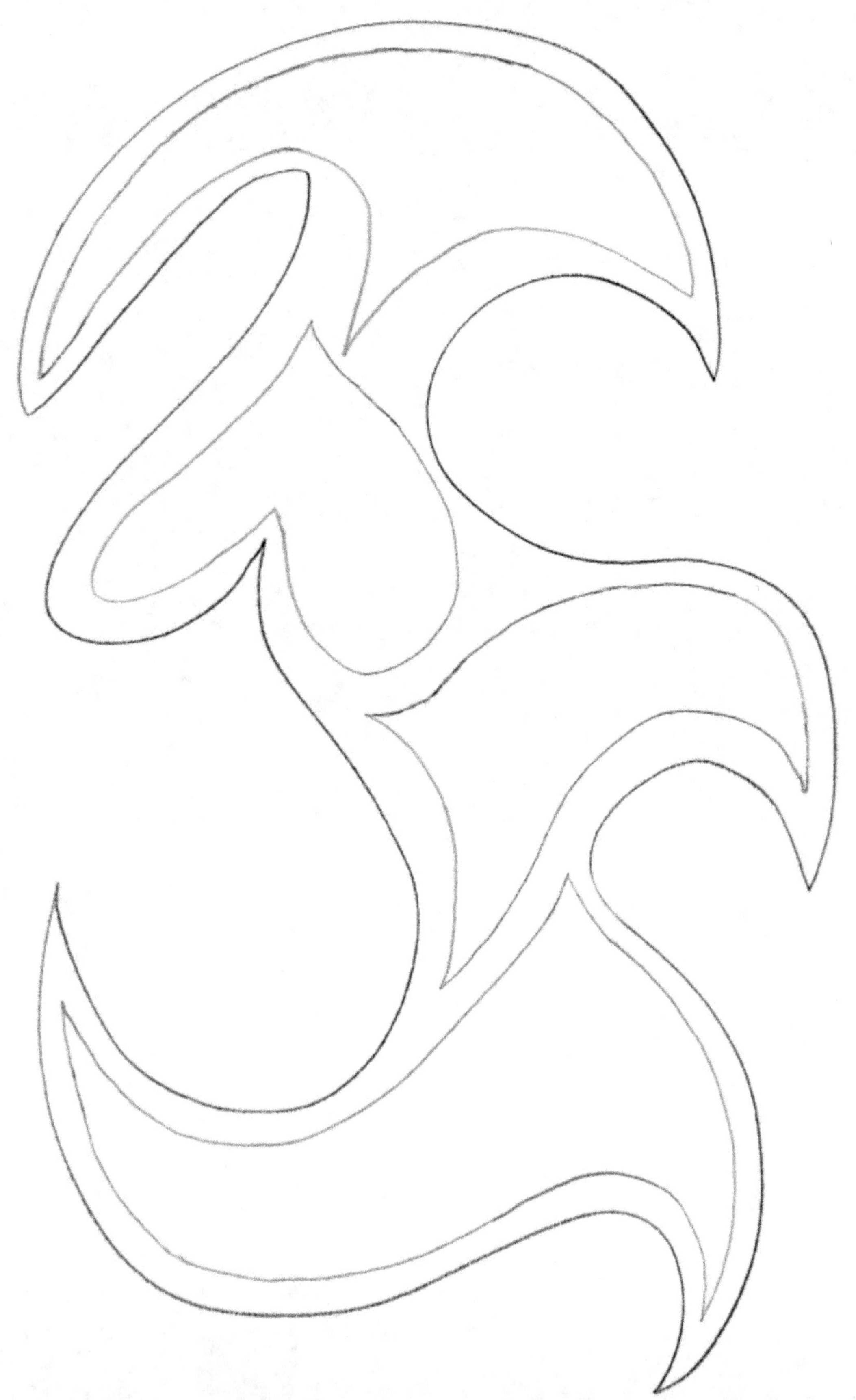

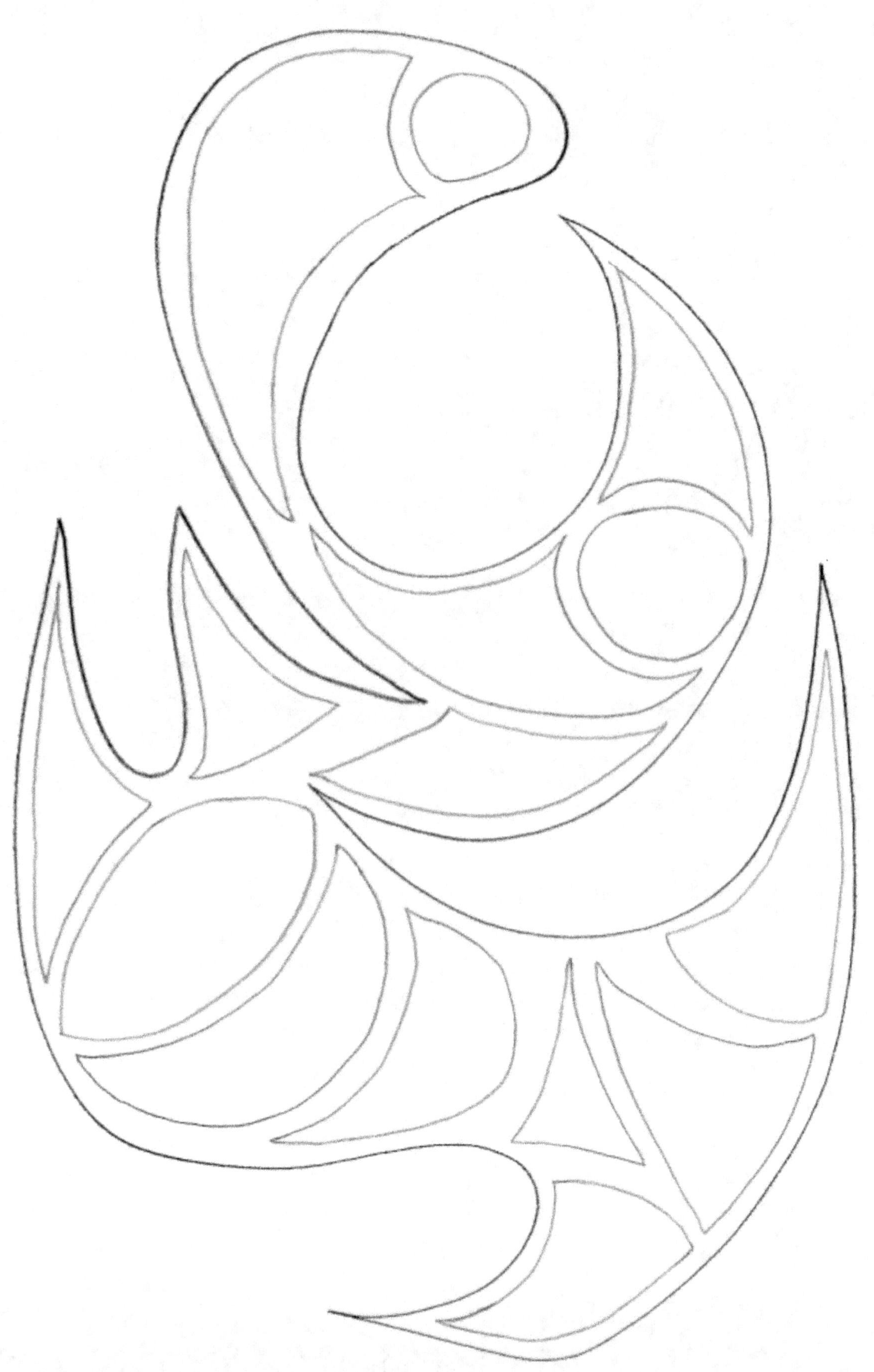

#11Cookies #ColorMeBrightCB

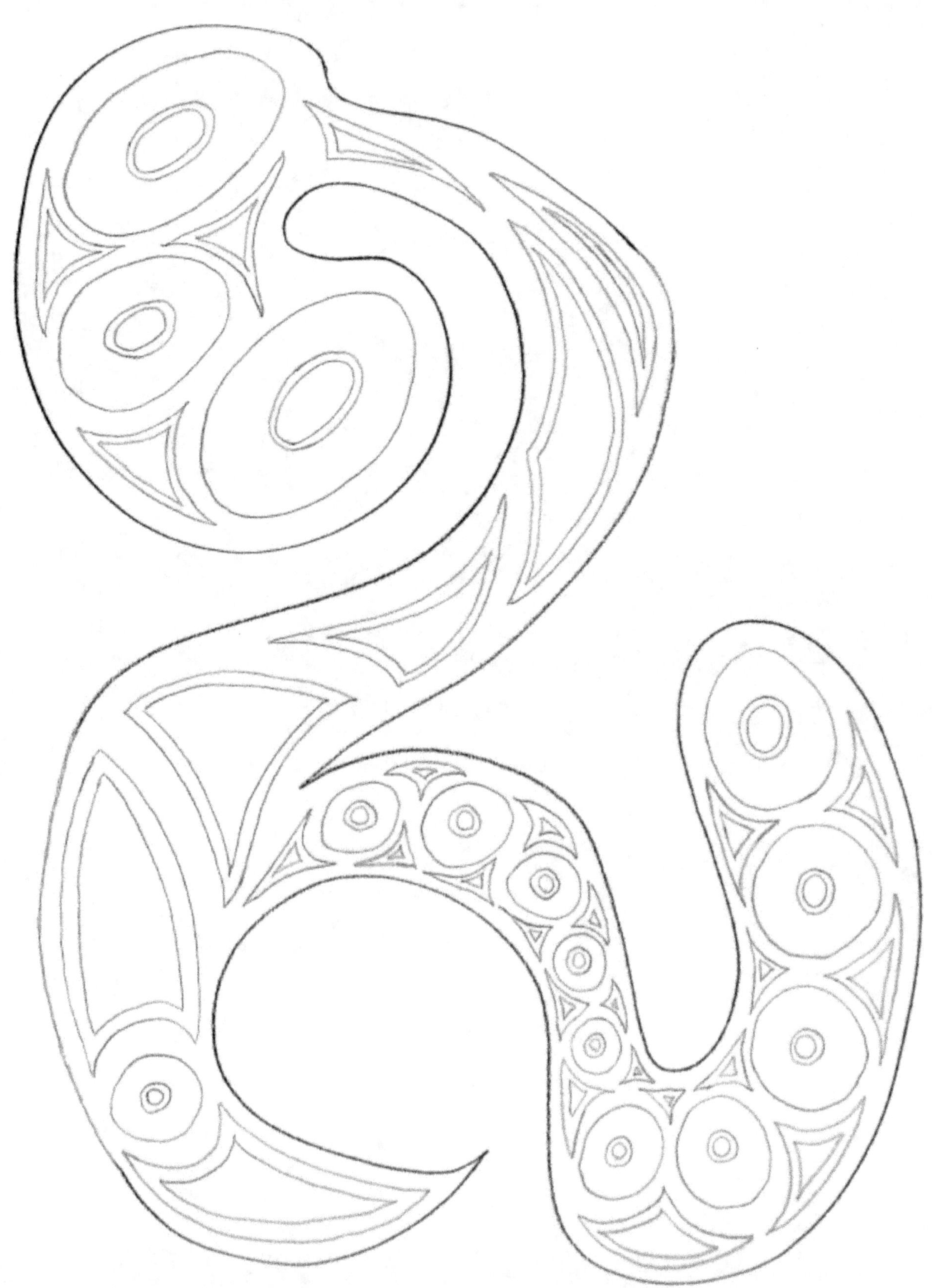

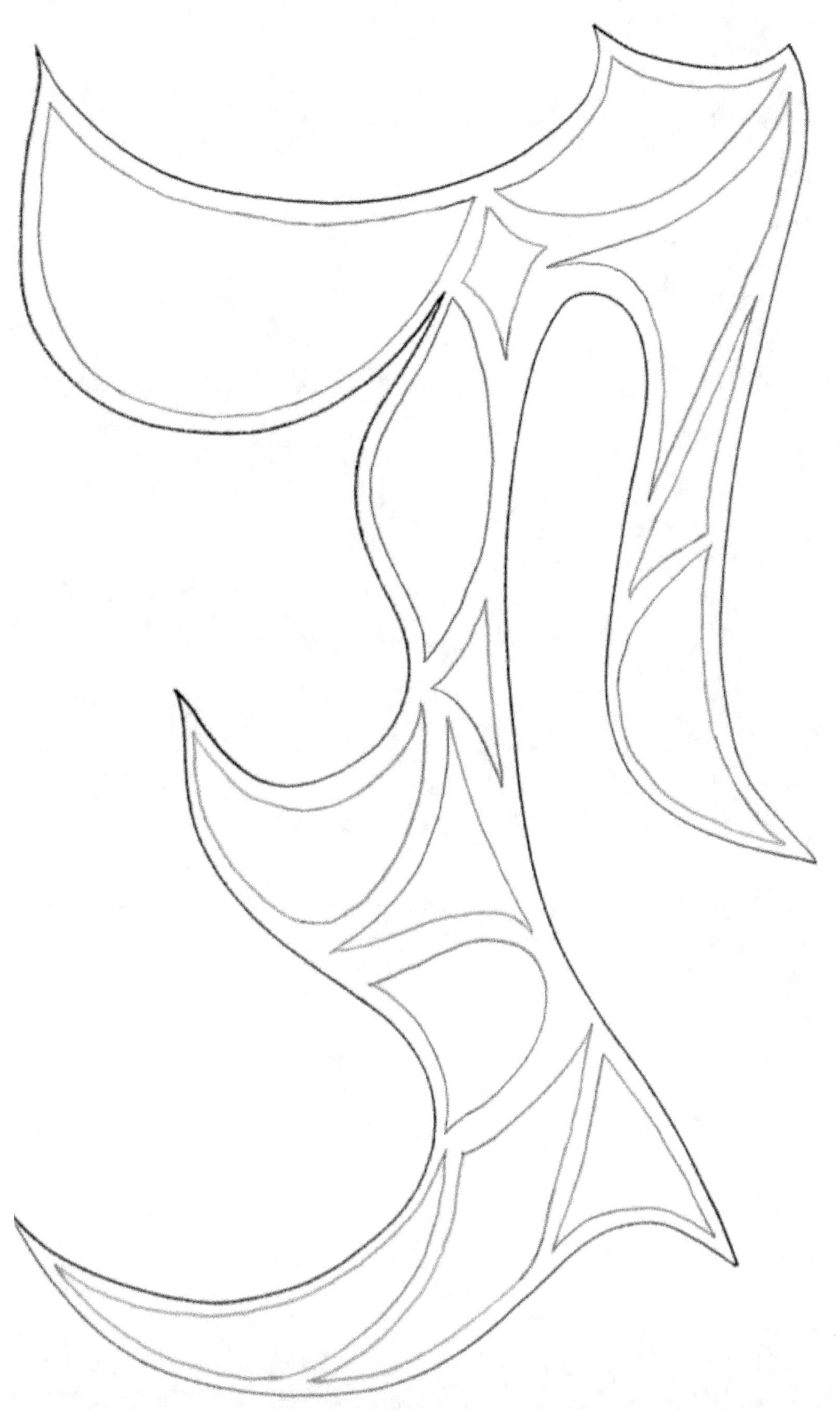

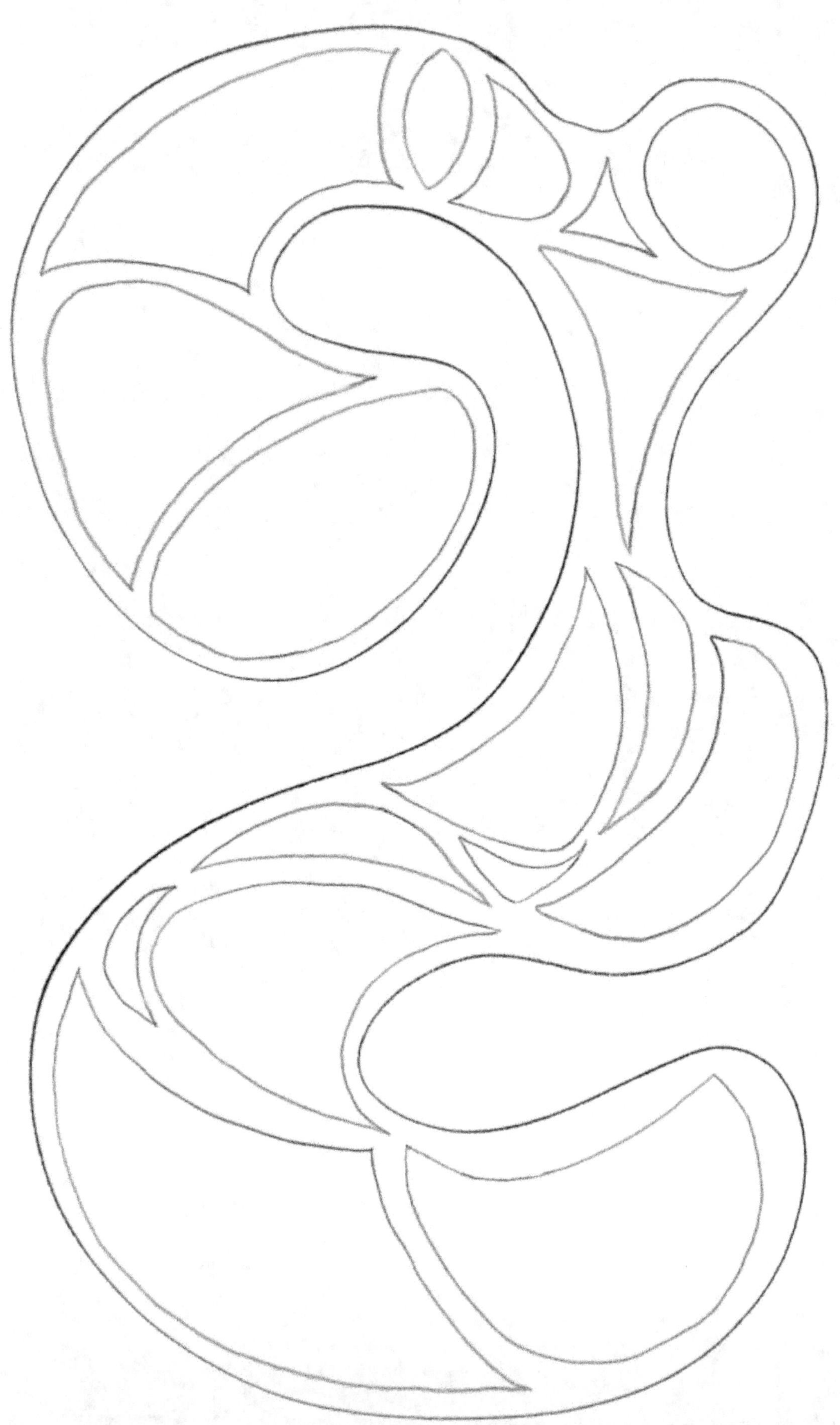

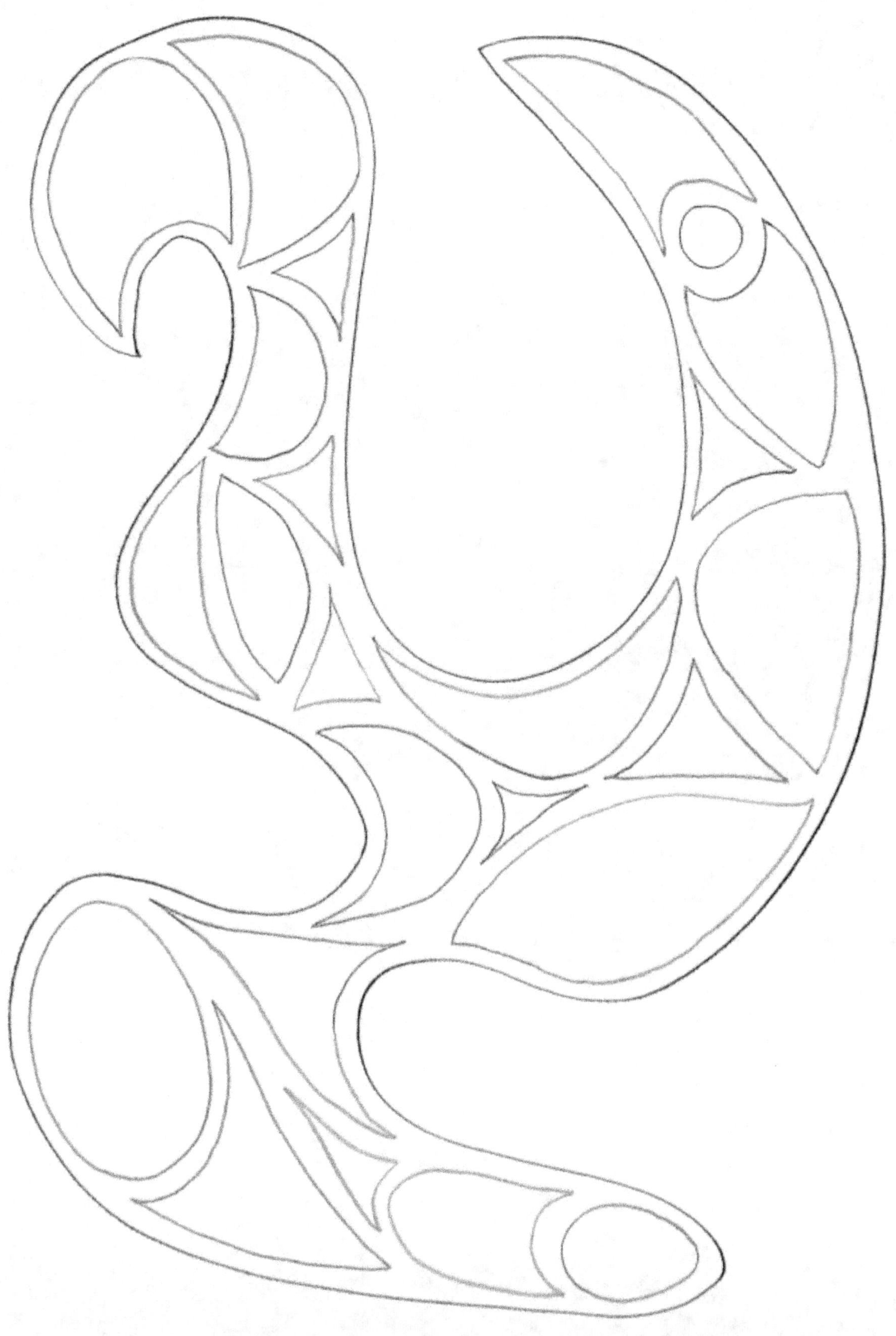

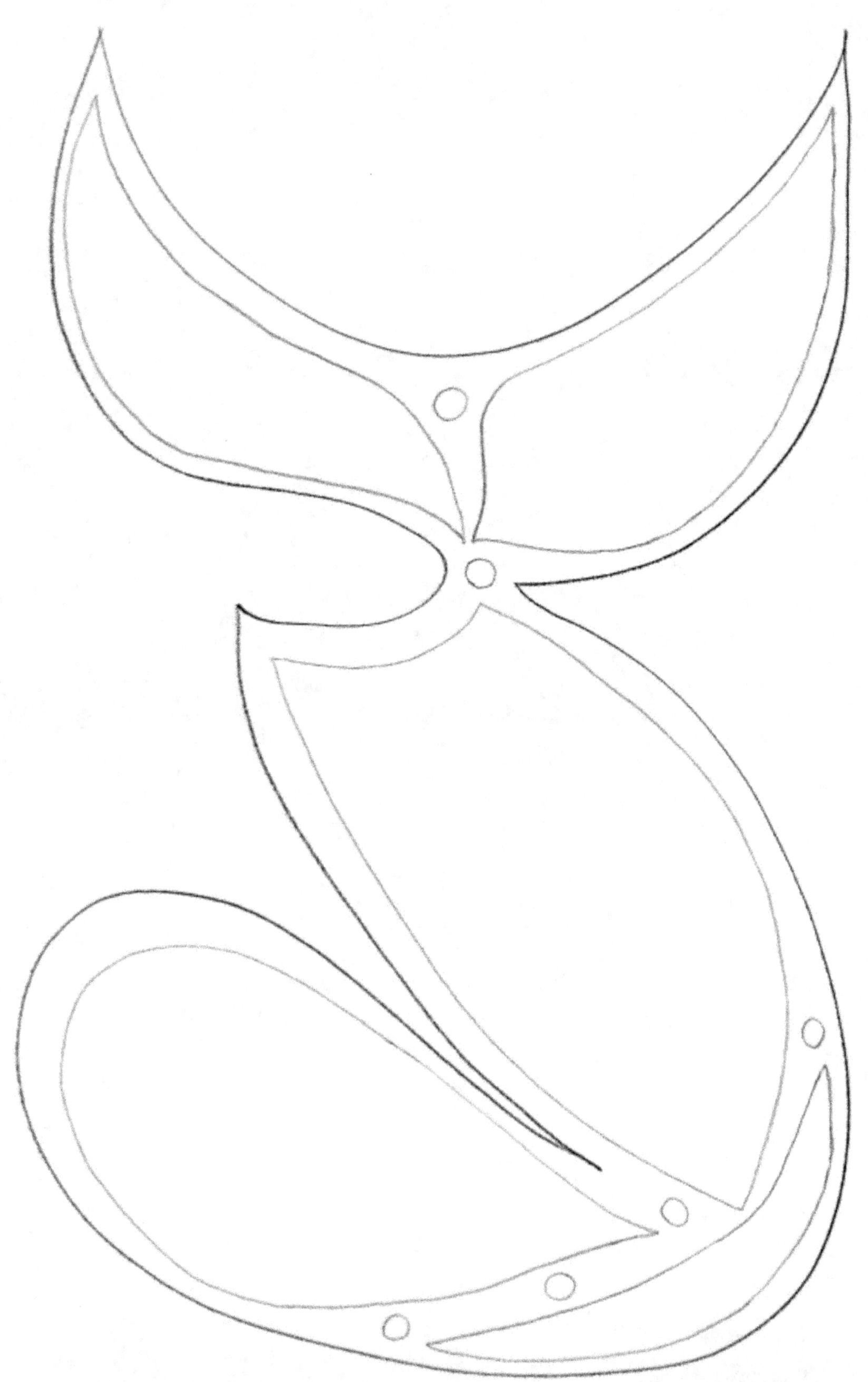

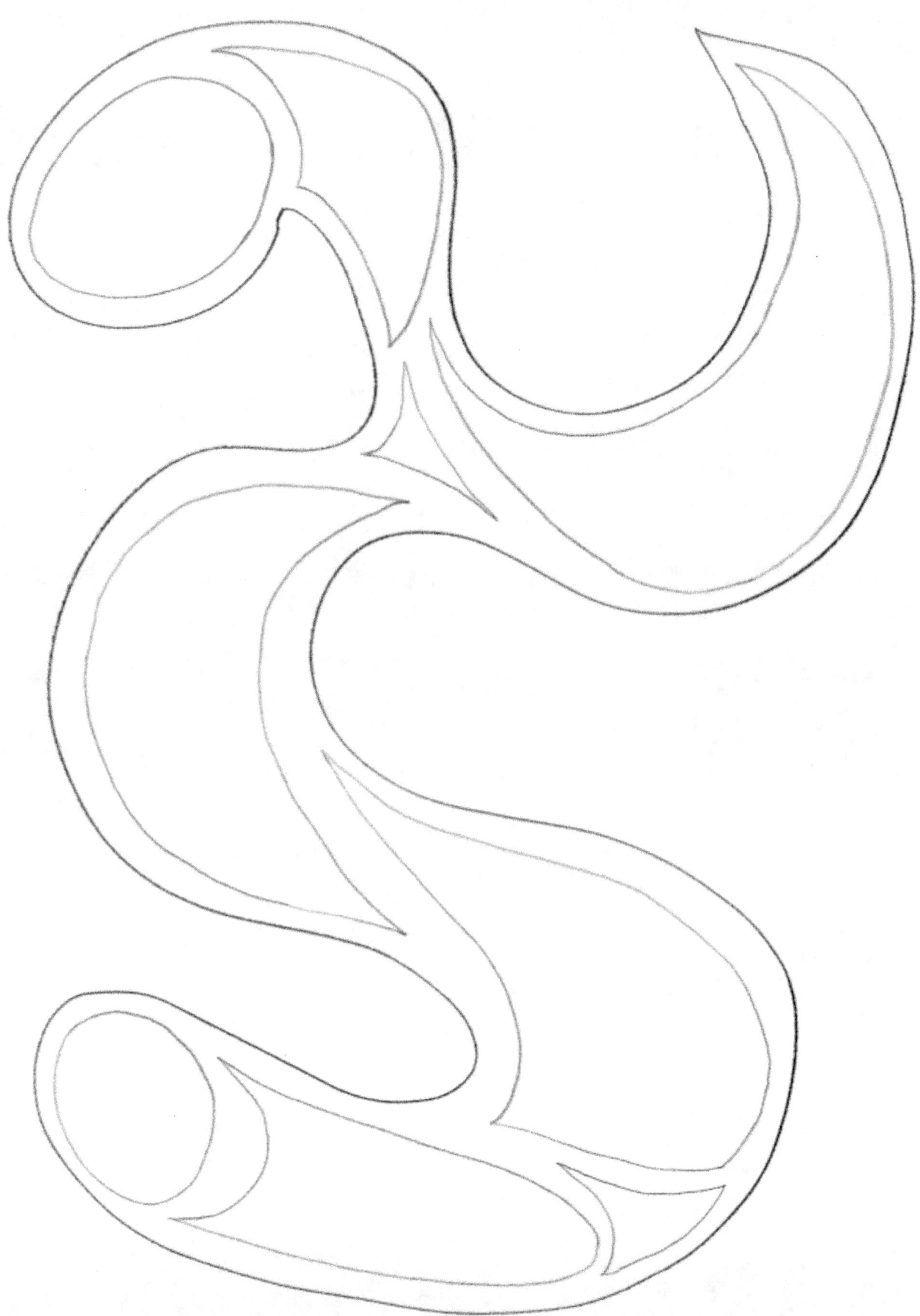

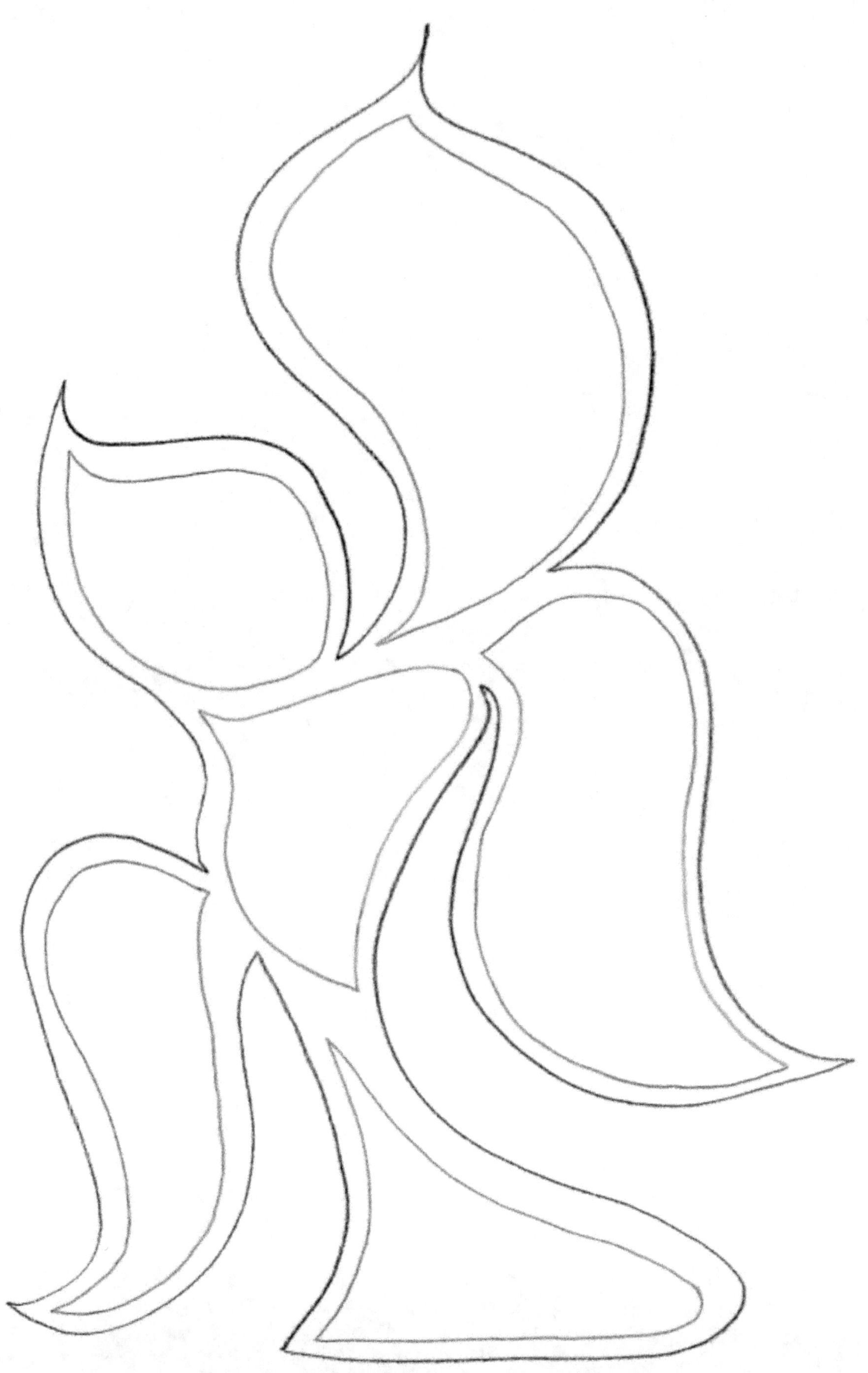

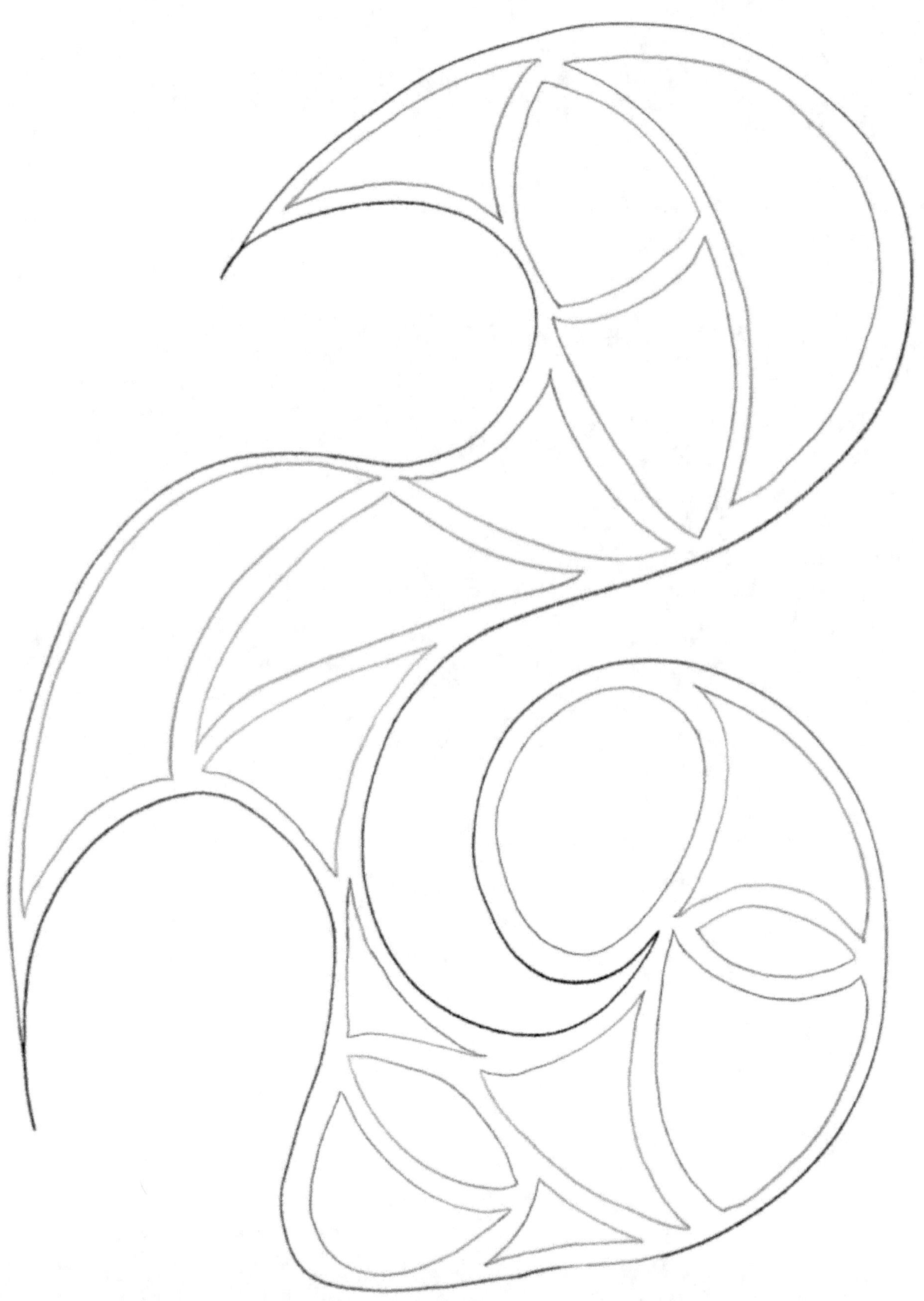

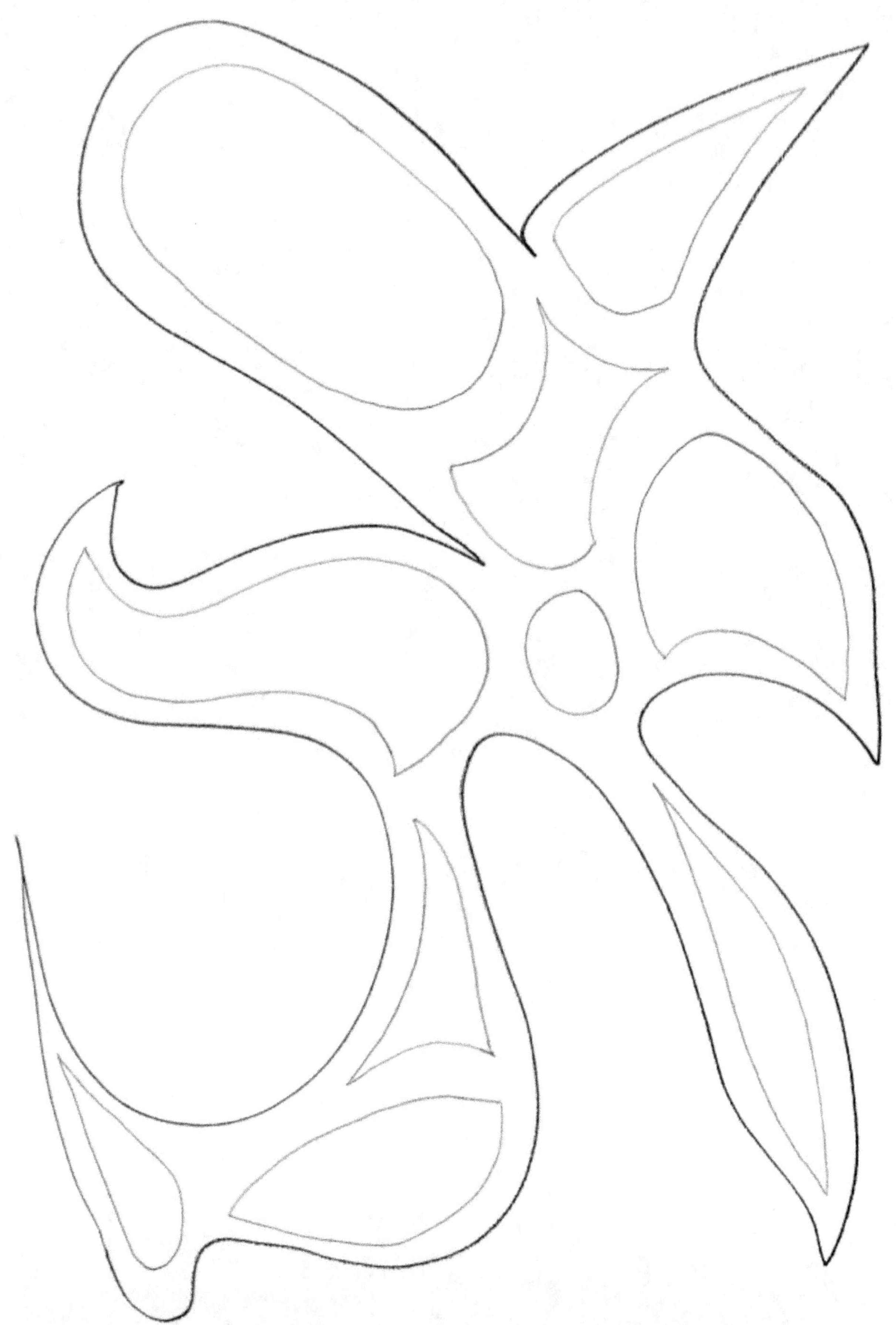

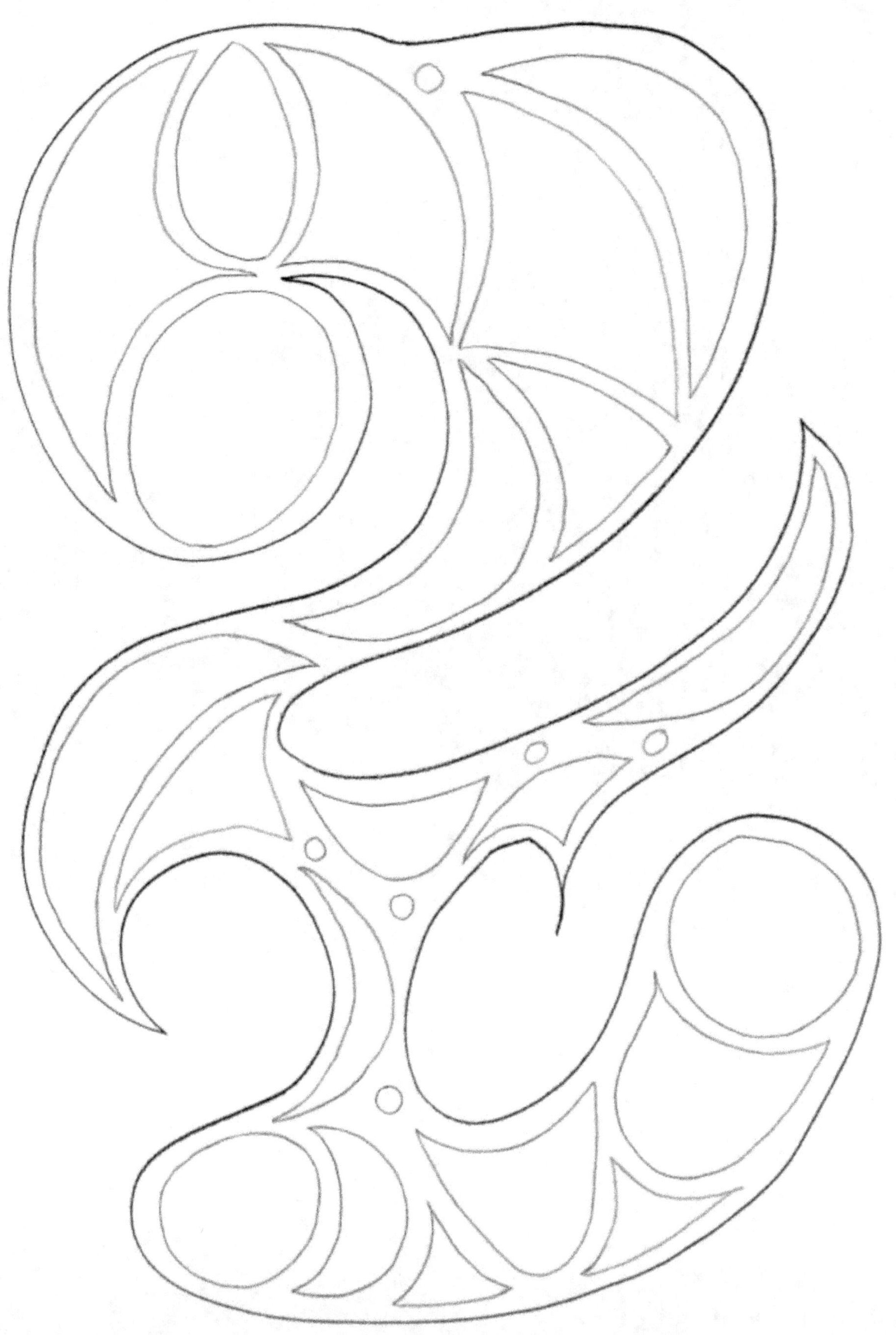

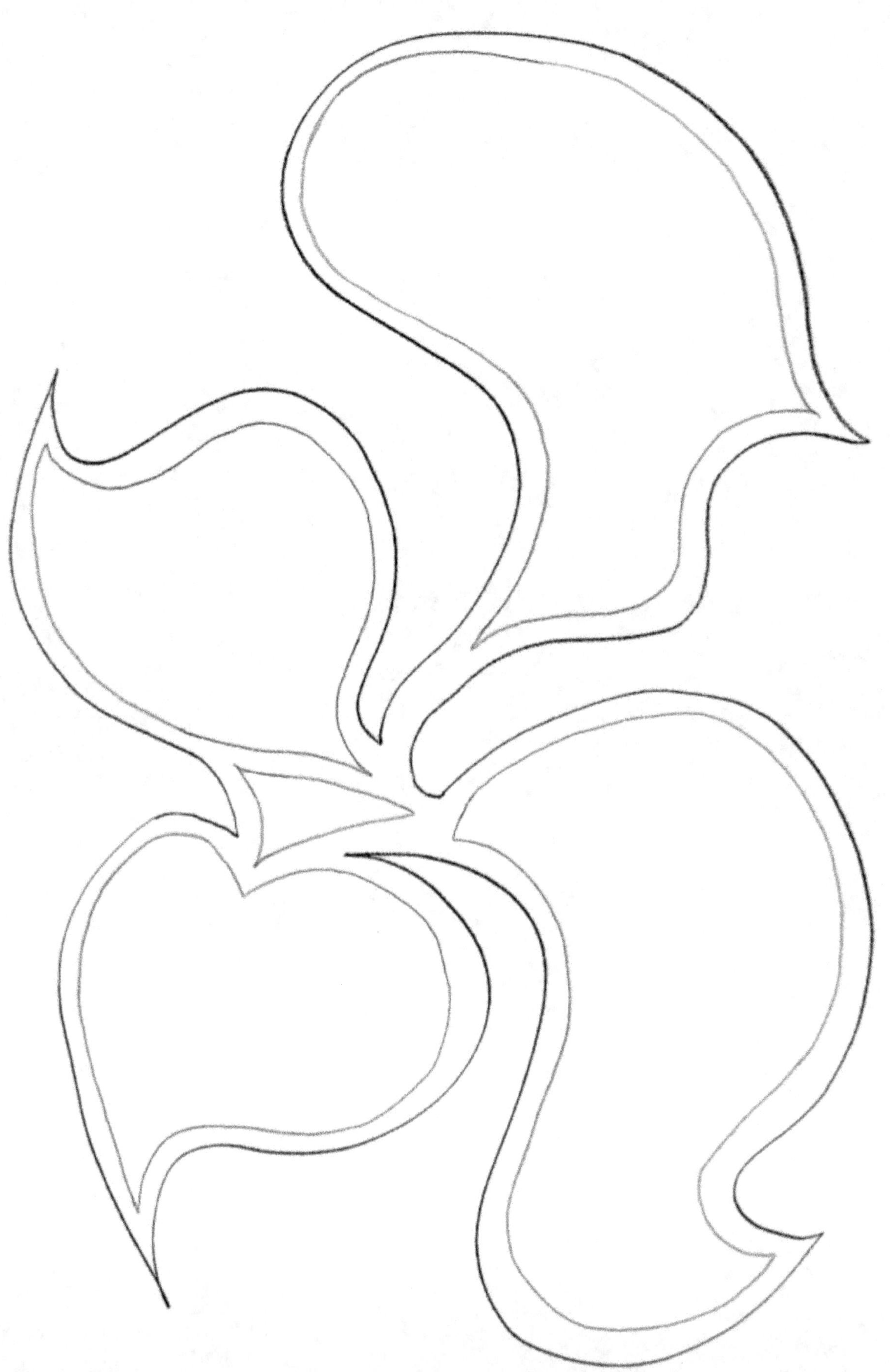

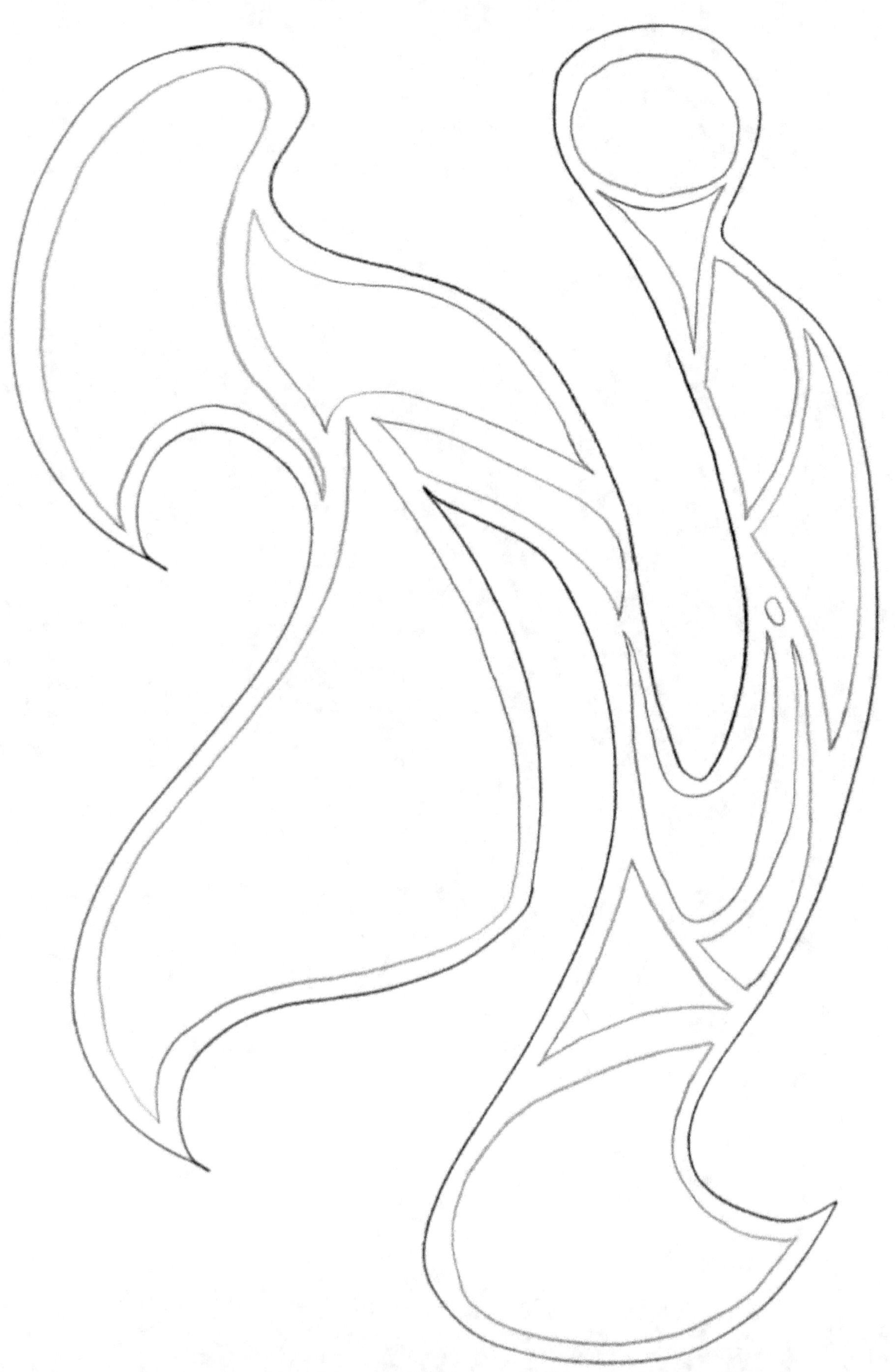

#23Hawks #ColorMeBrightCB

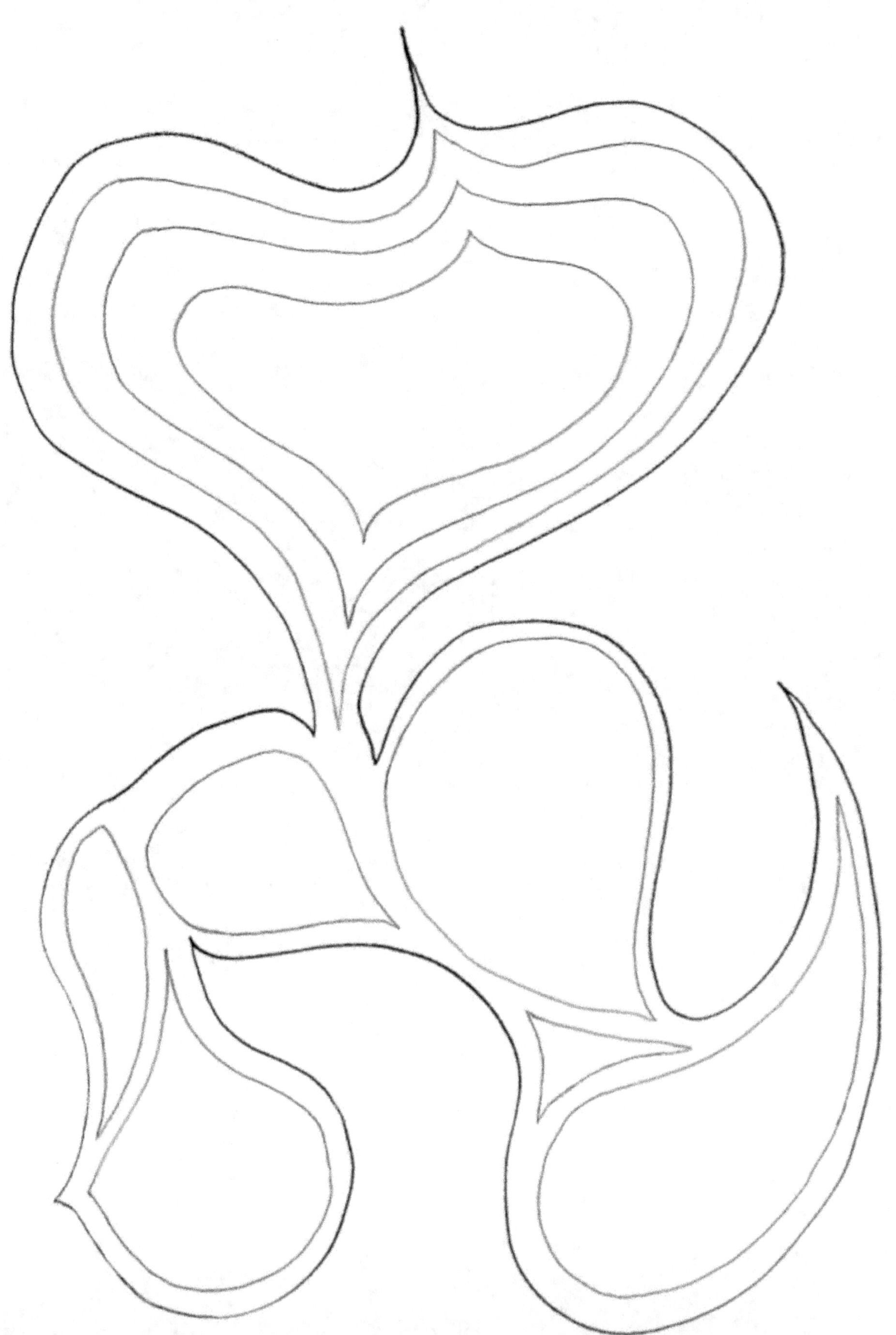

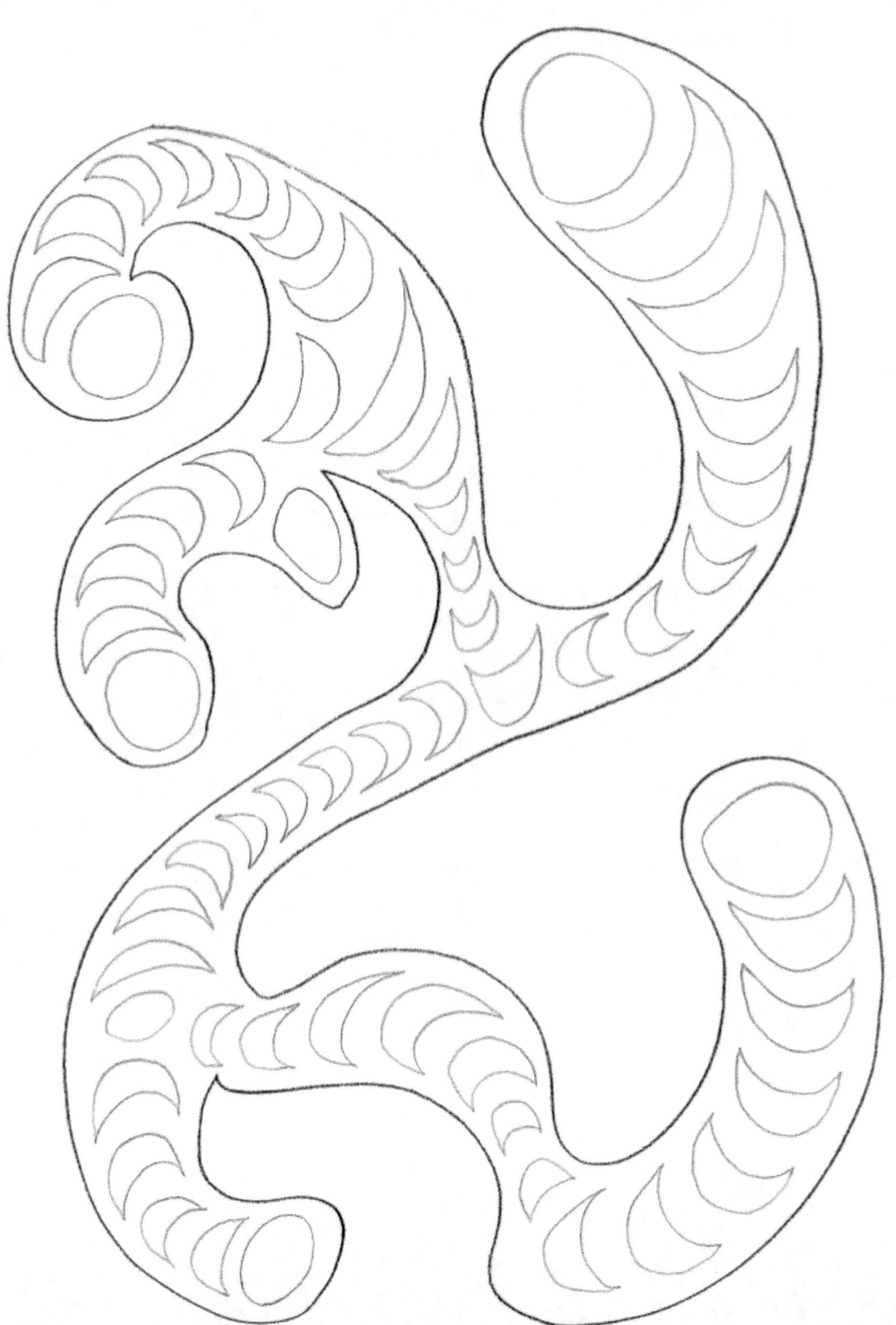

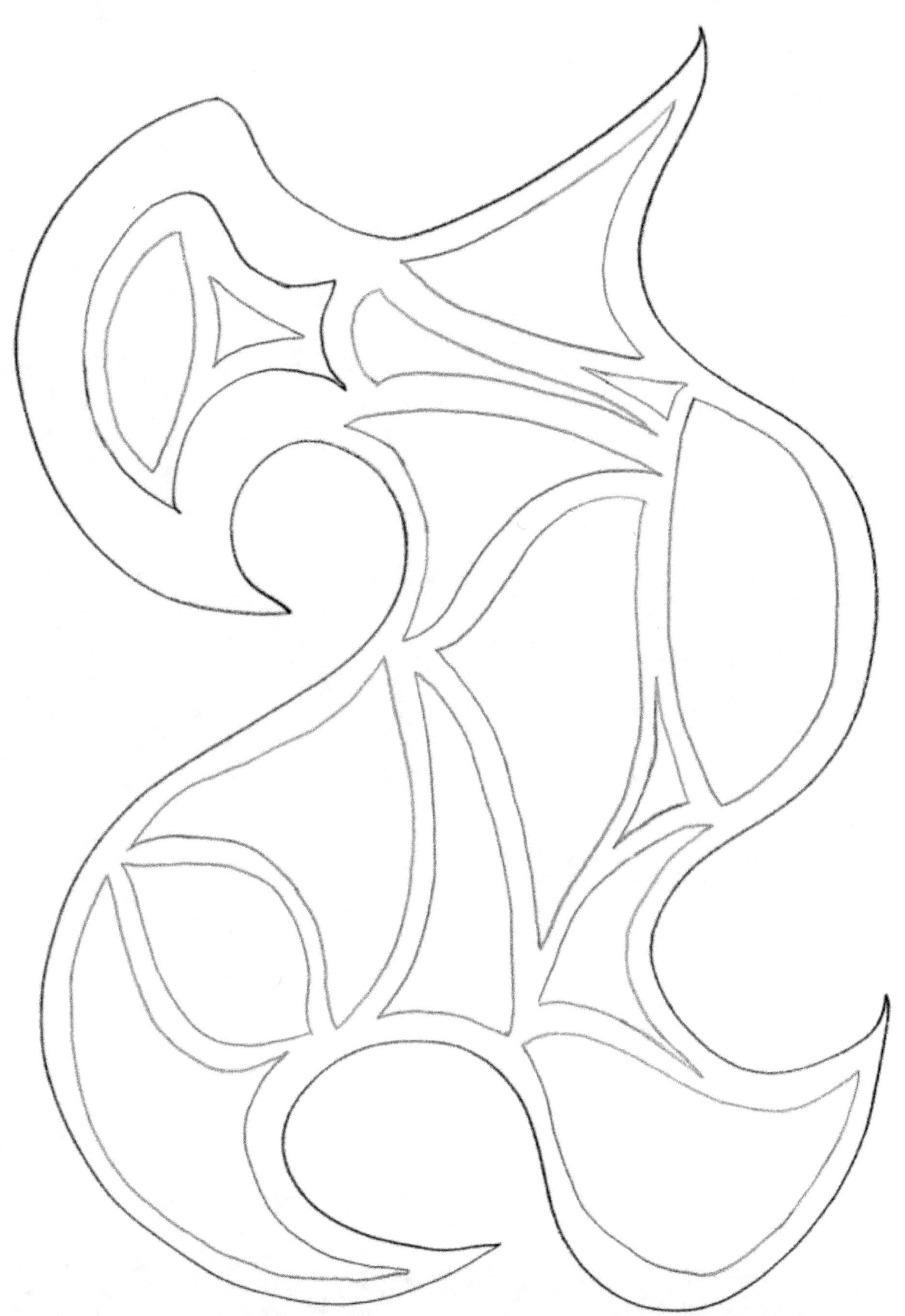

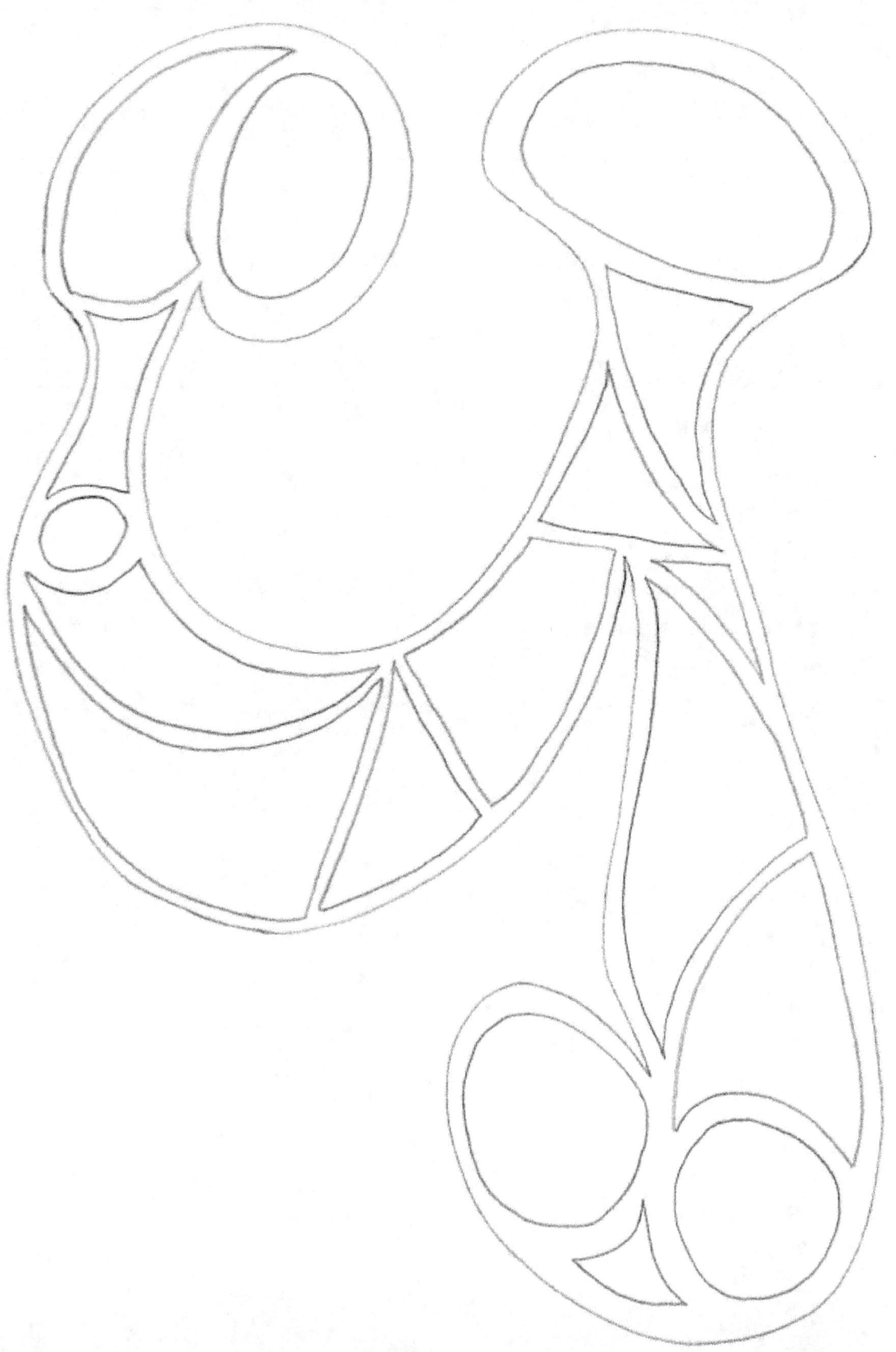

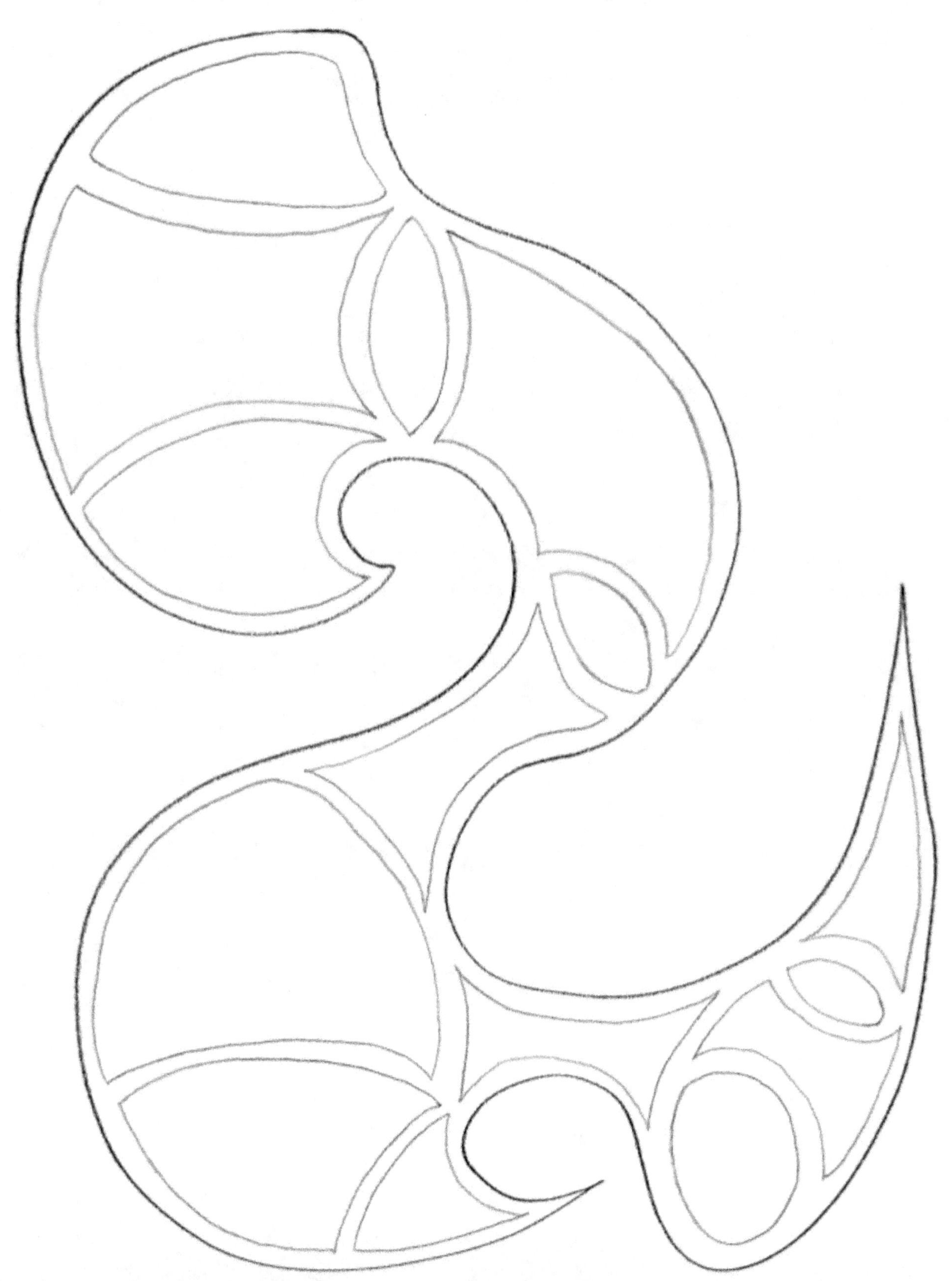

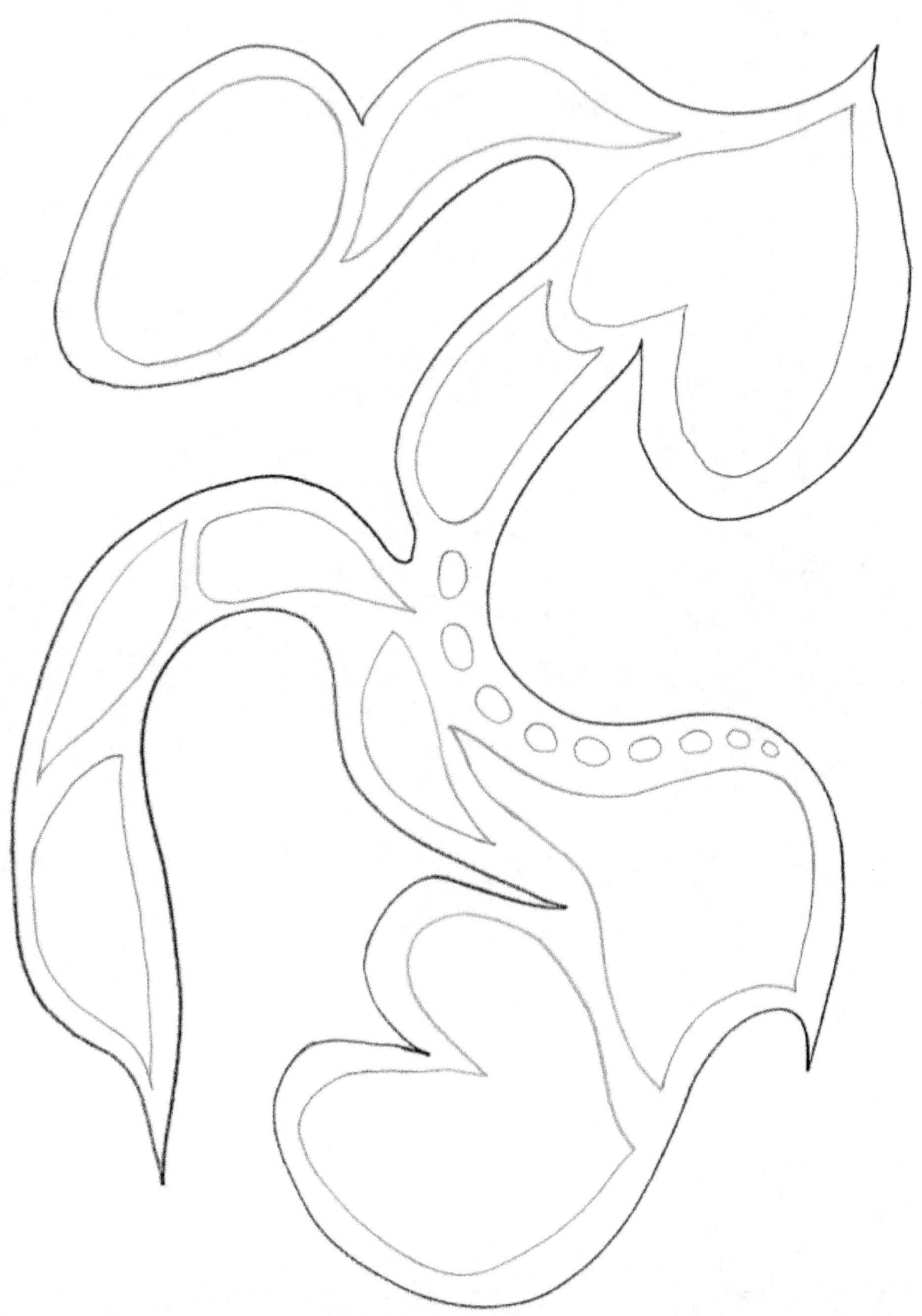

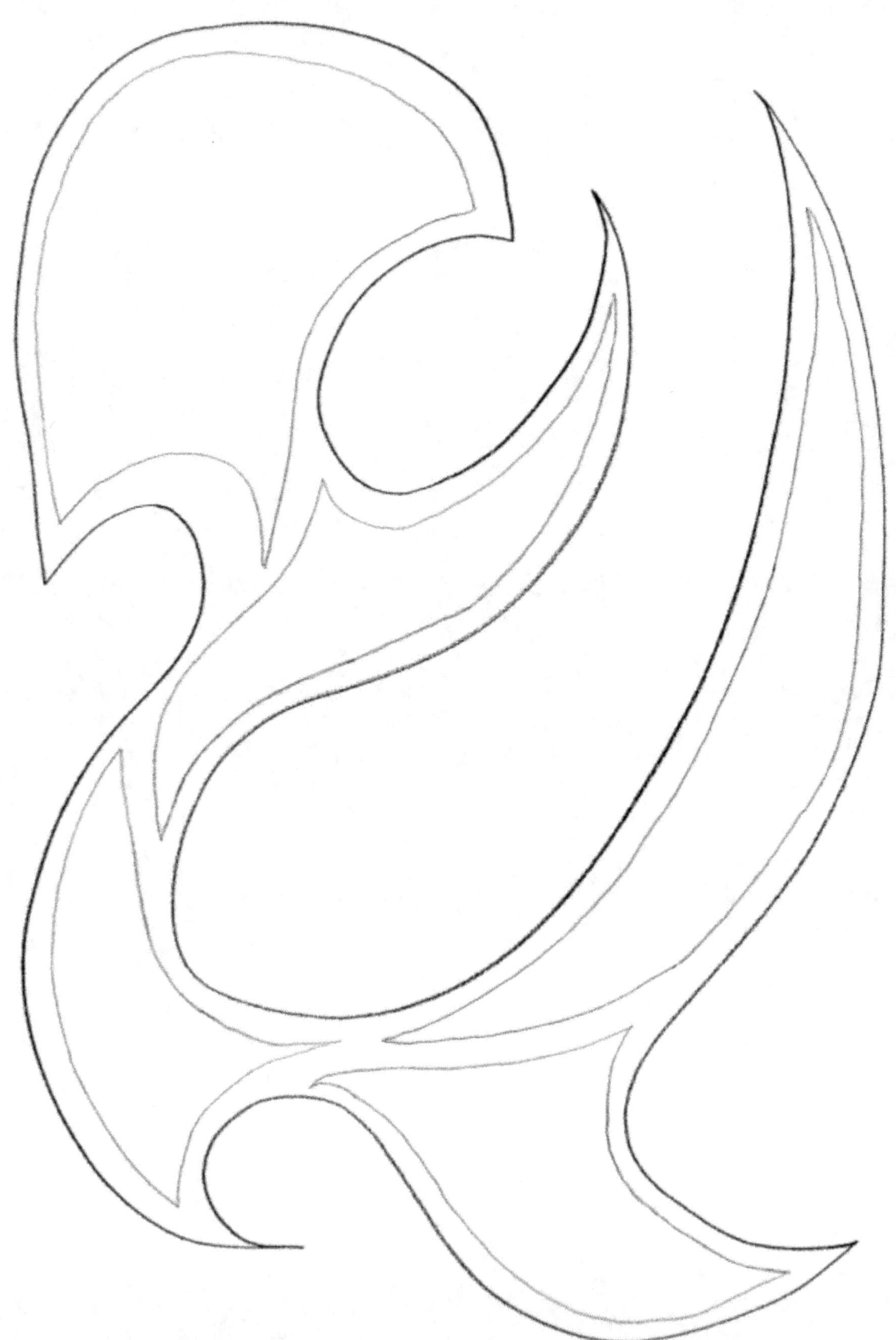

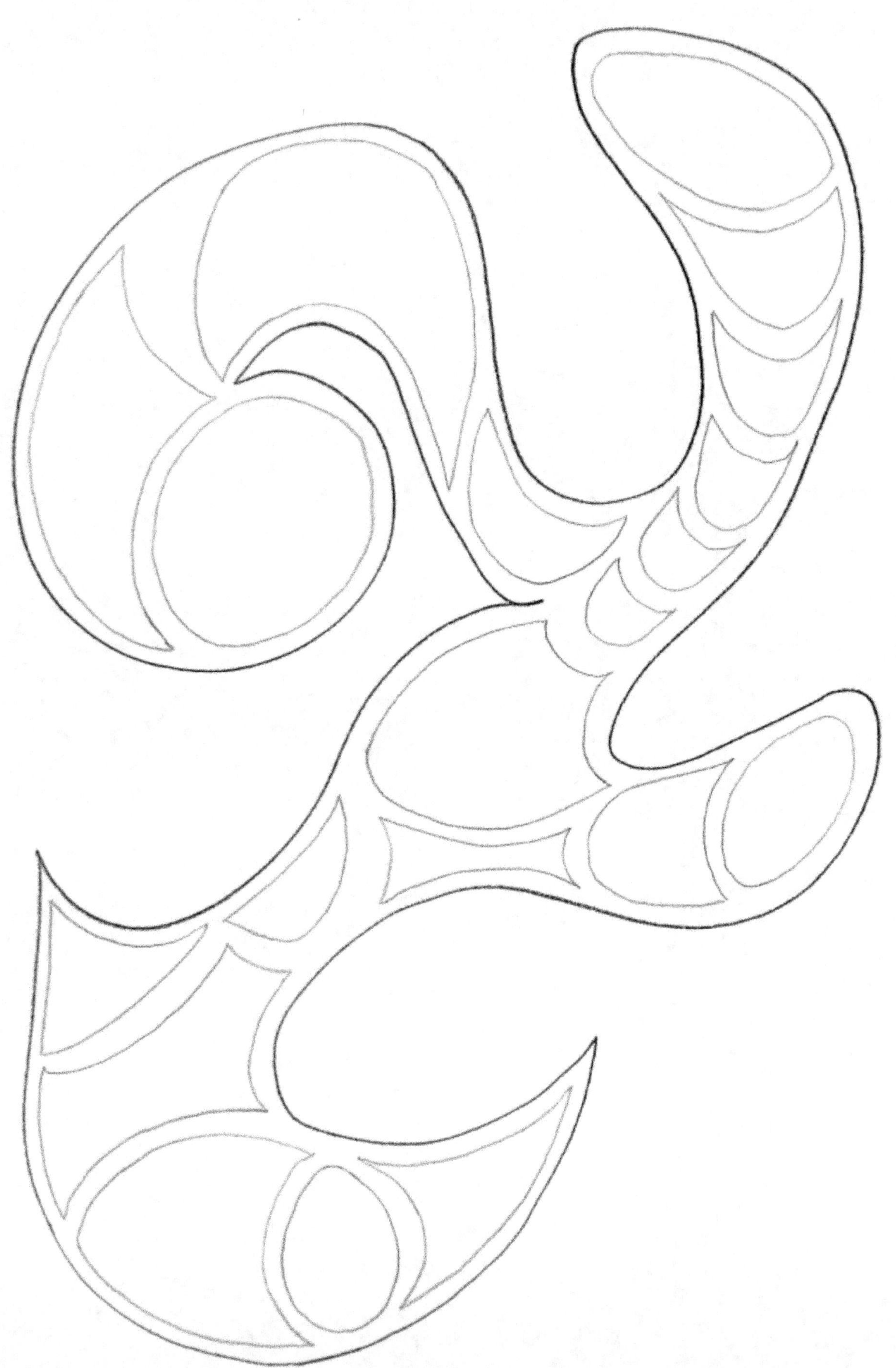

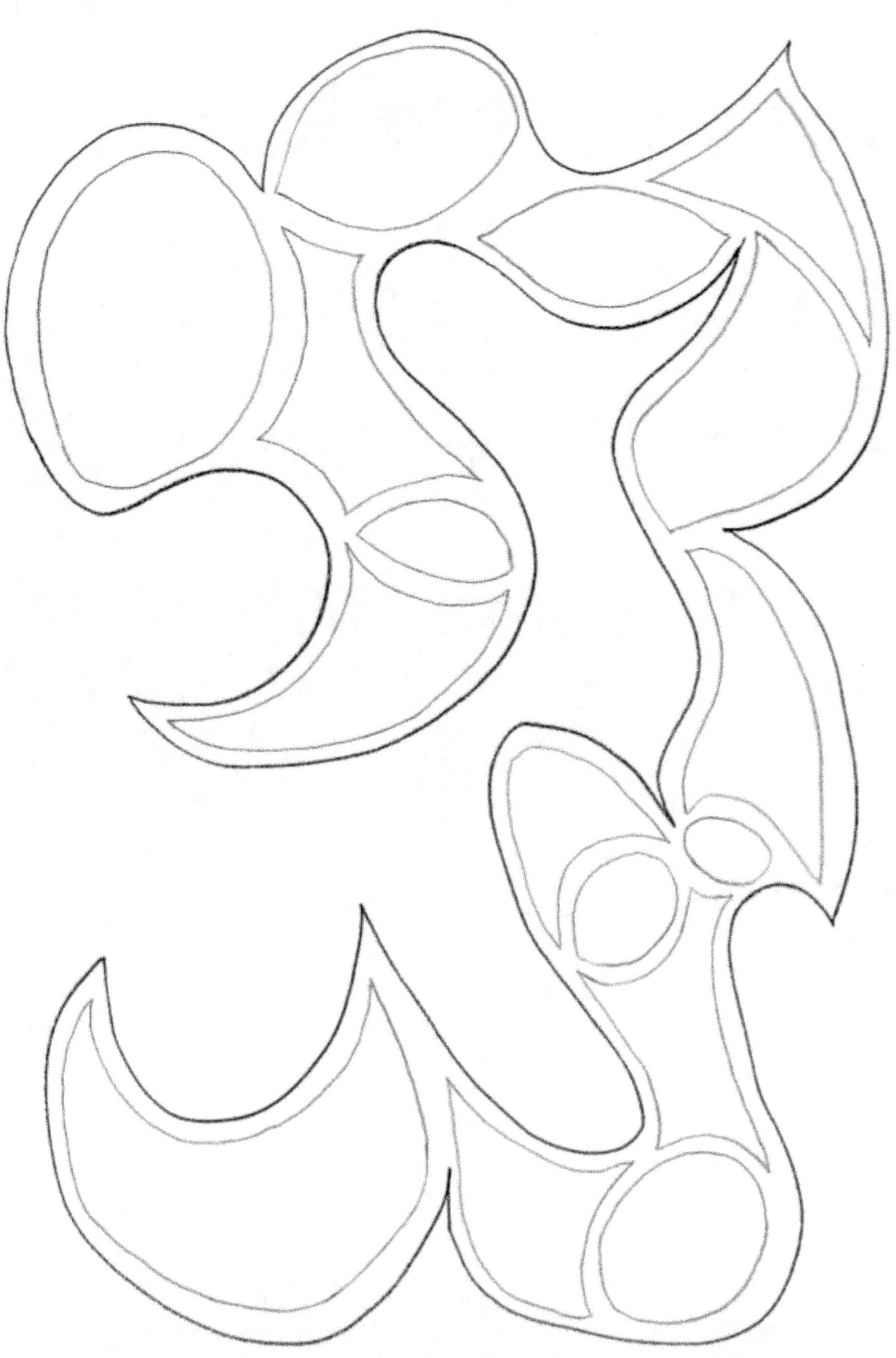

#32Peacocks #ColorMeBrightCB

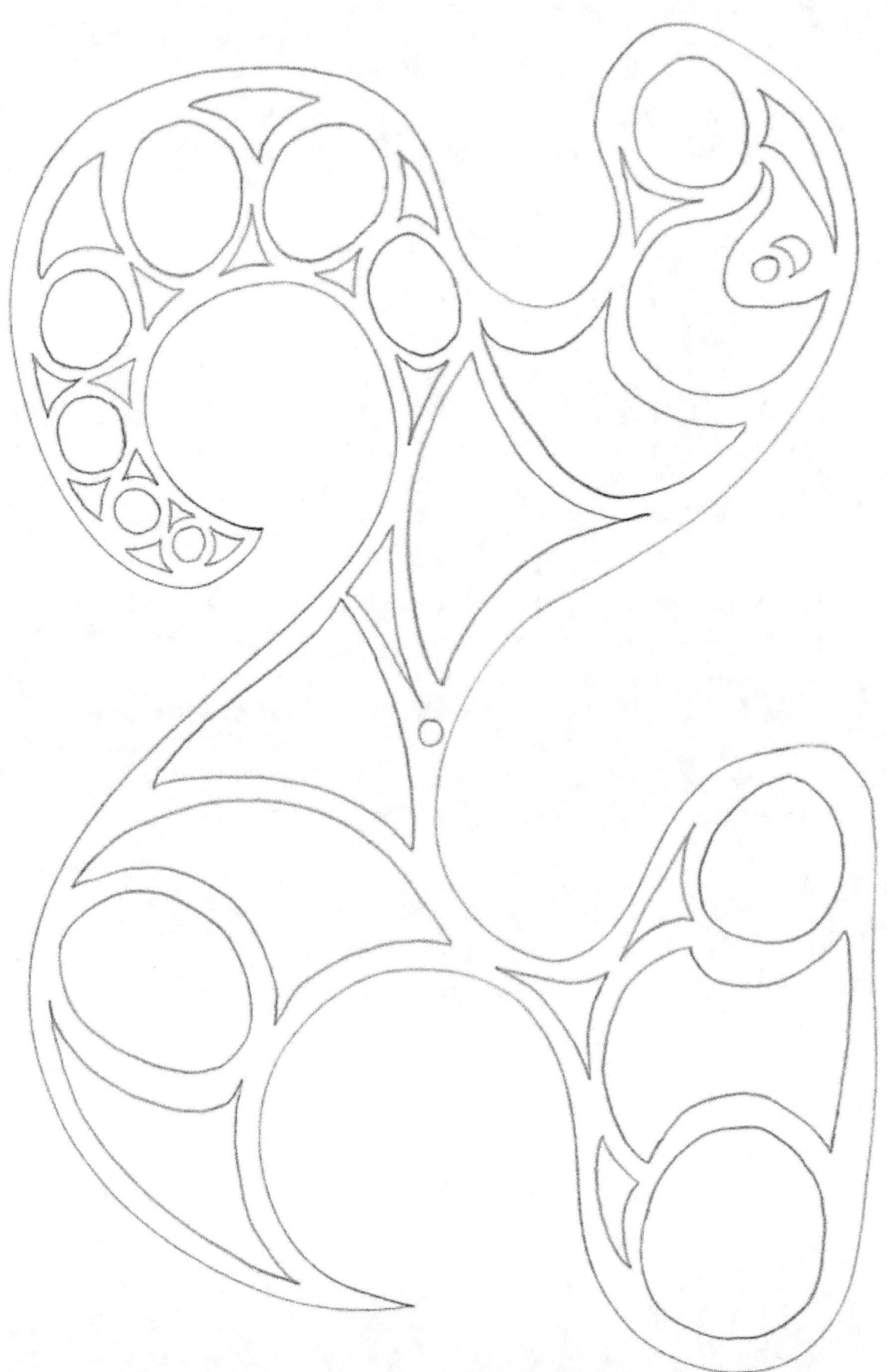

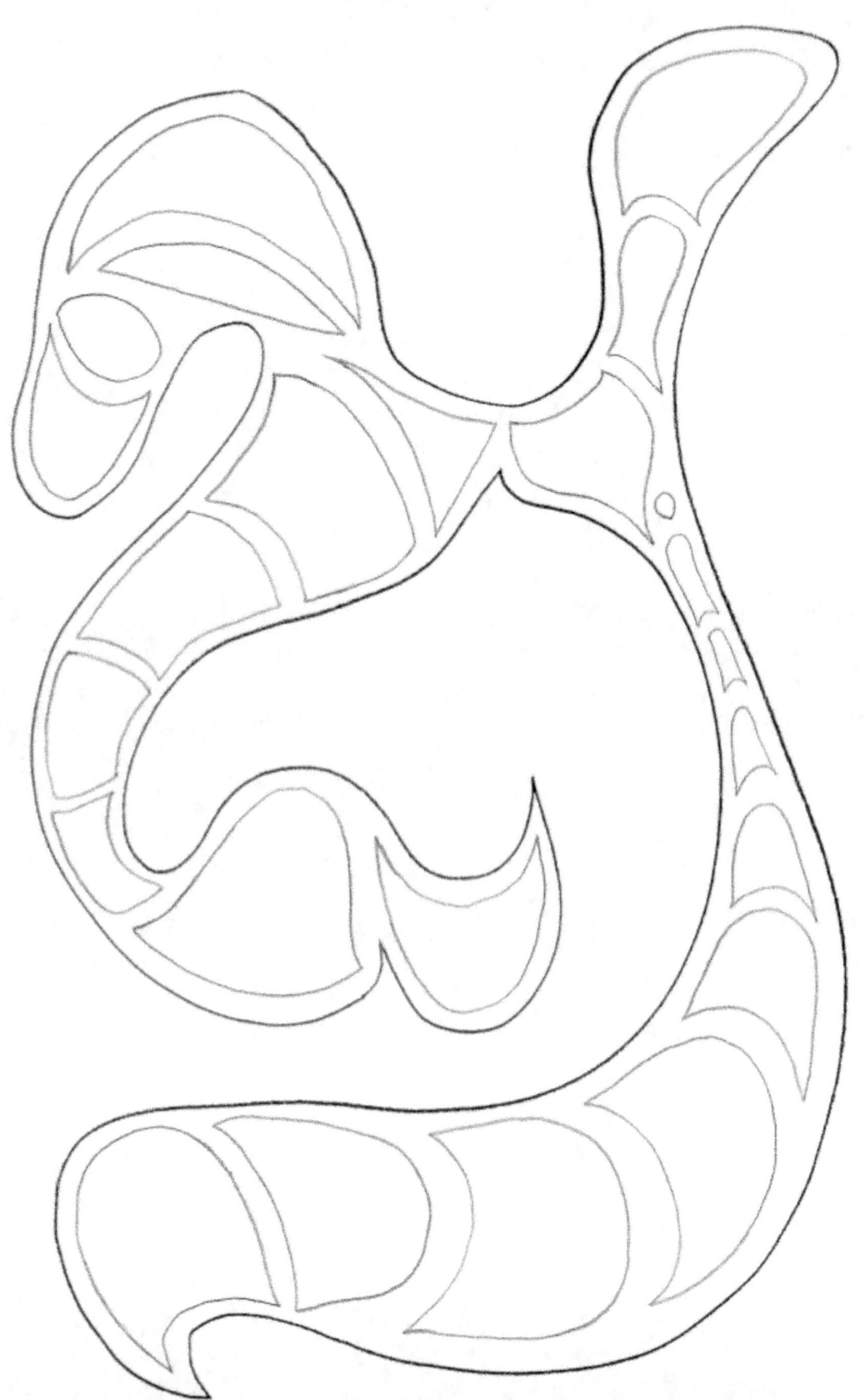

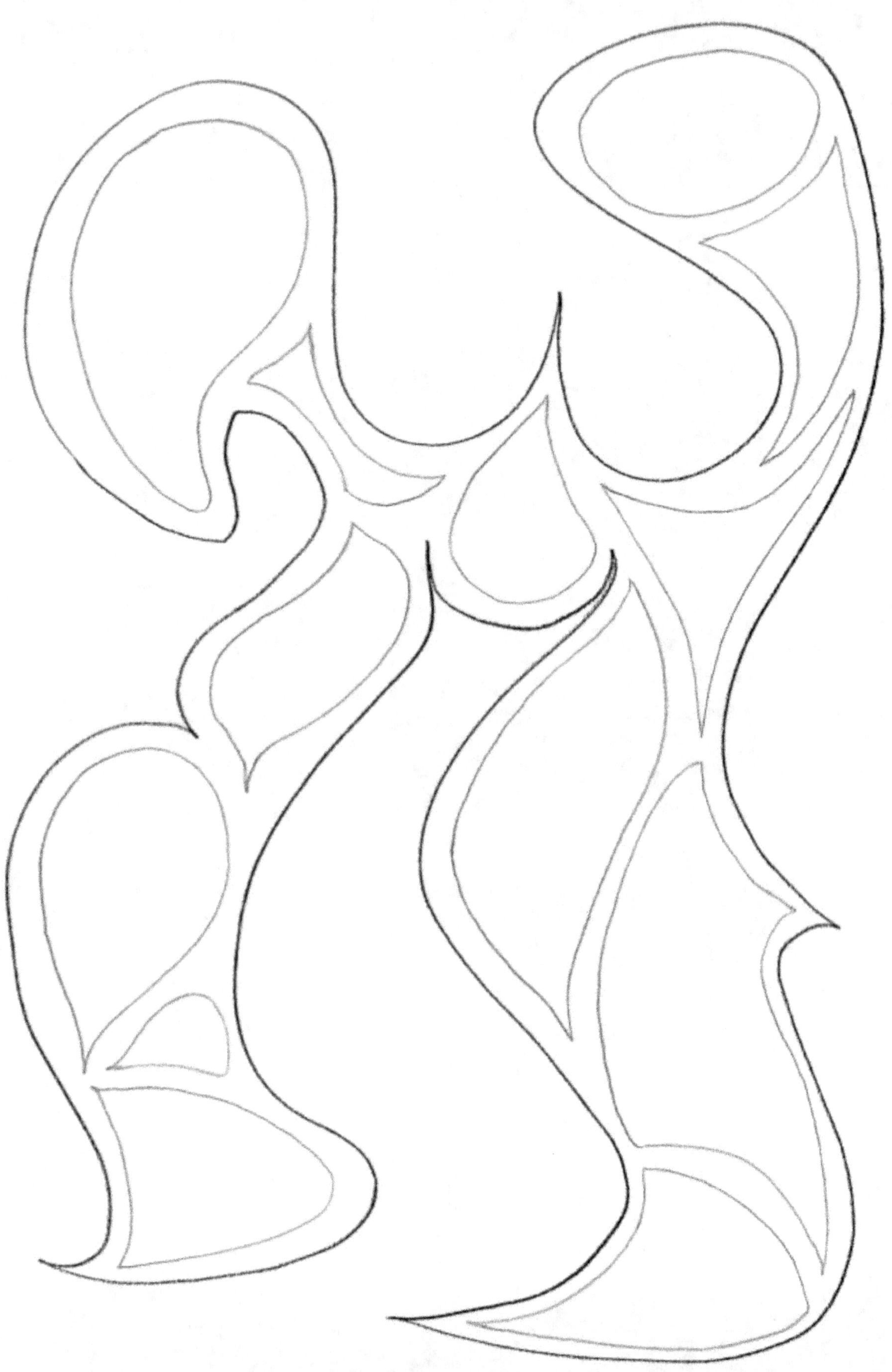

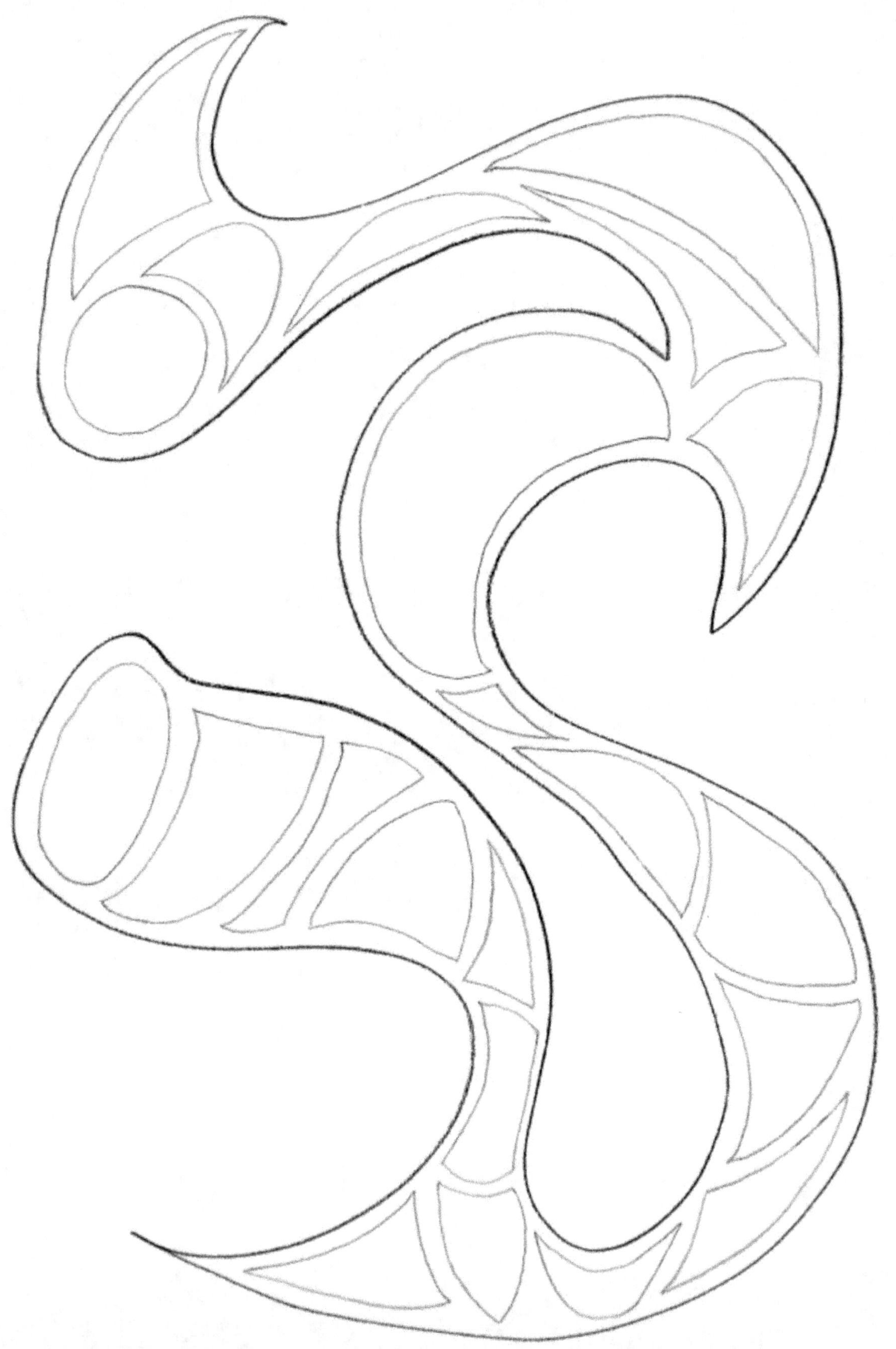

#36Popcorn #ColorMeBrightCB

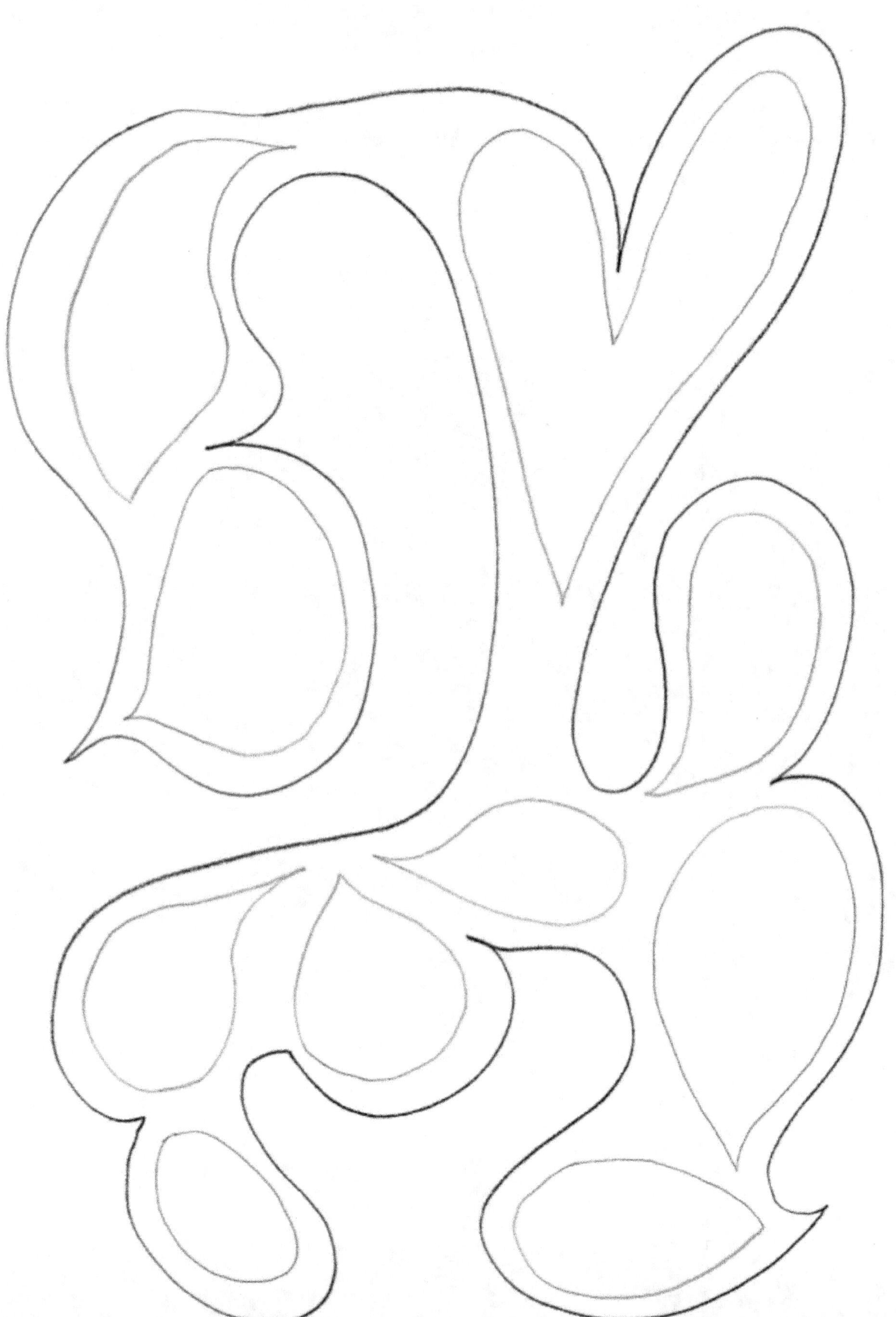

#37Popsicle #ColorMeBrightCB

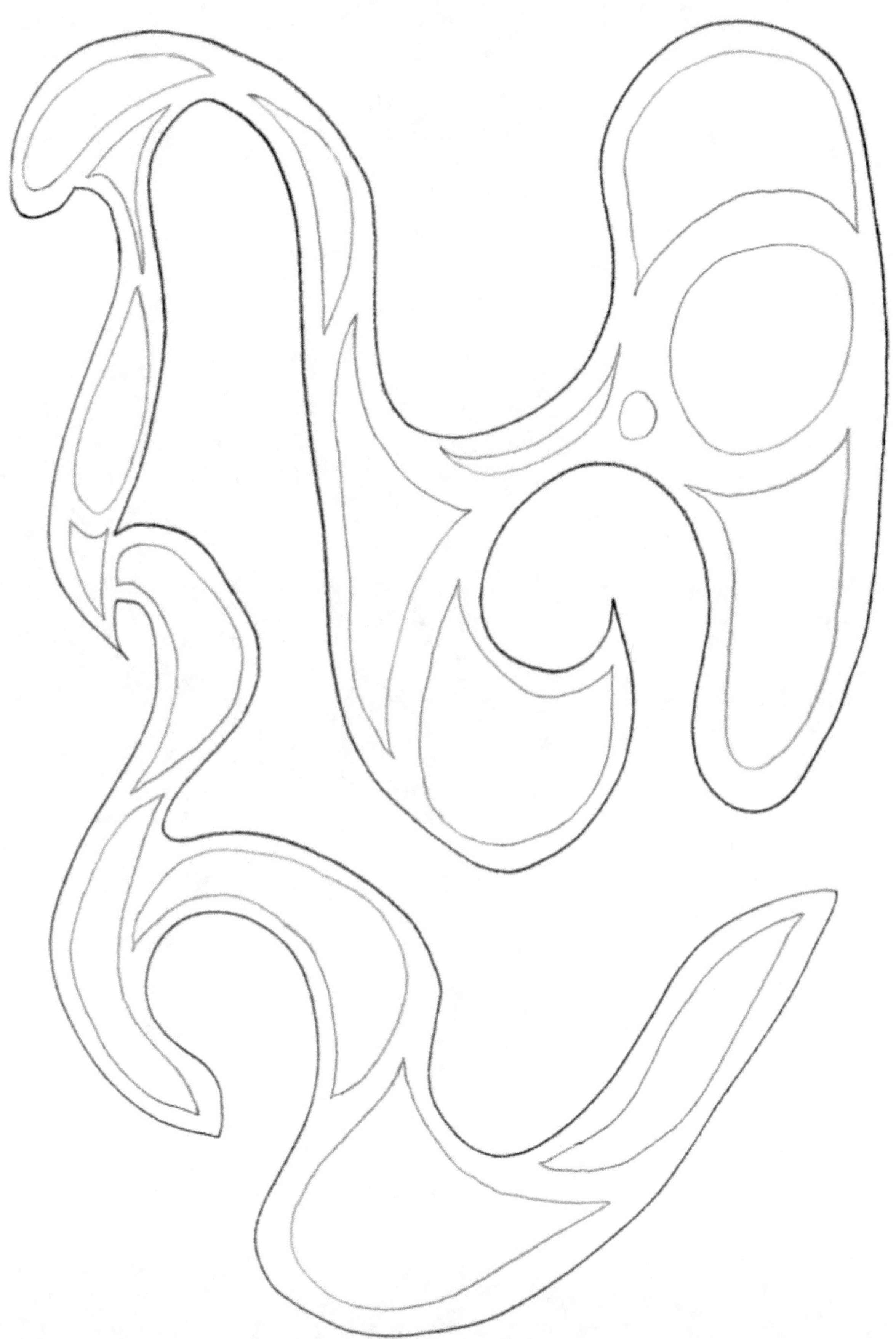

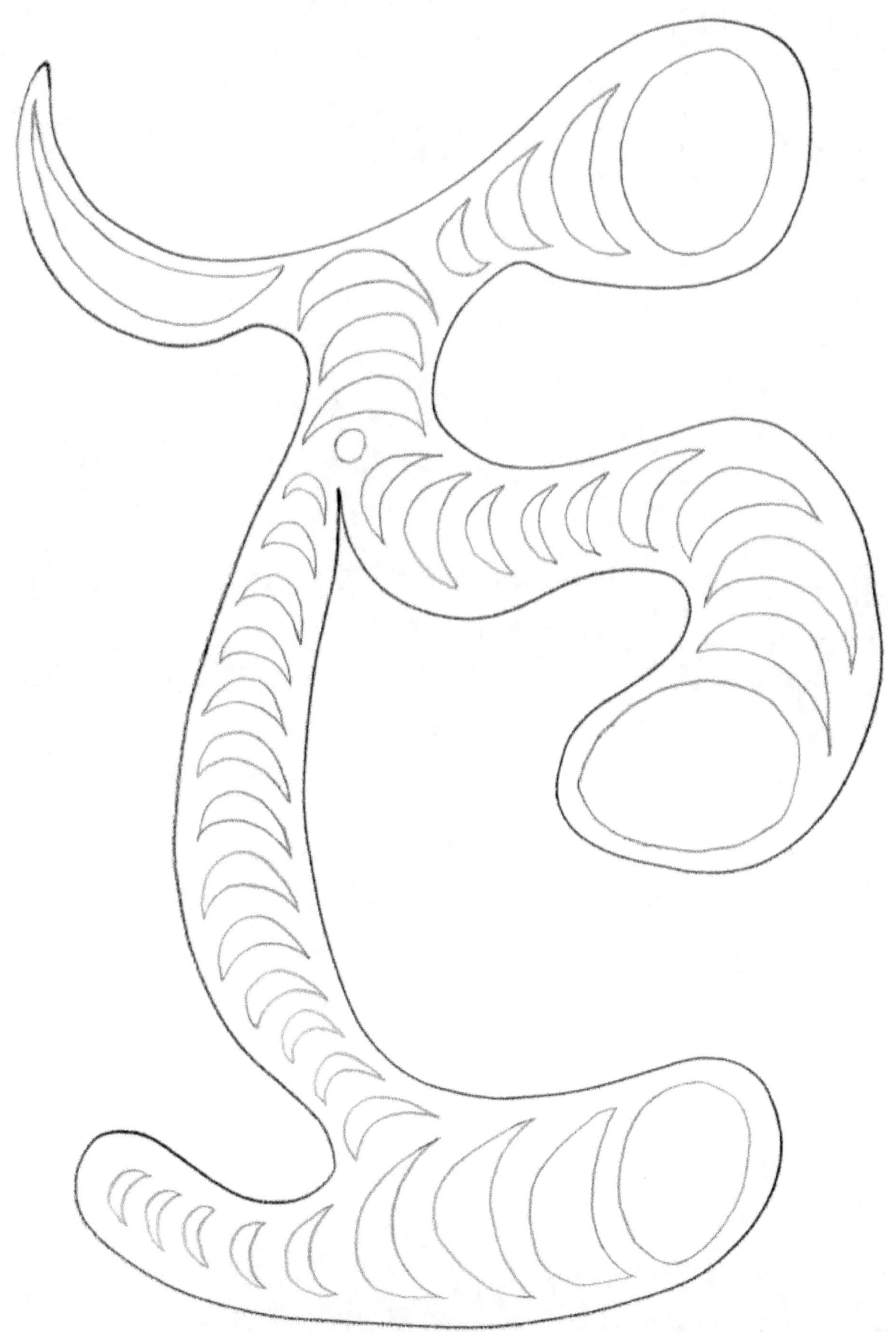

#39Quartz #ColorMeBrightCB

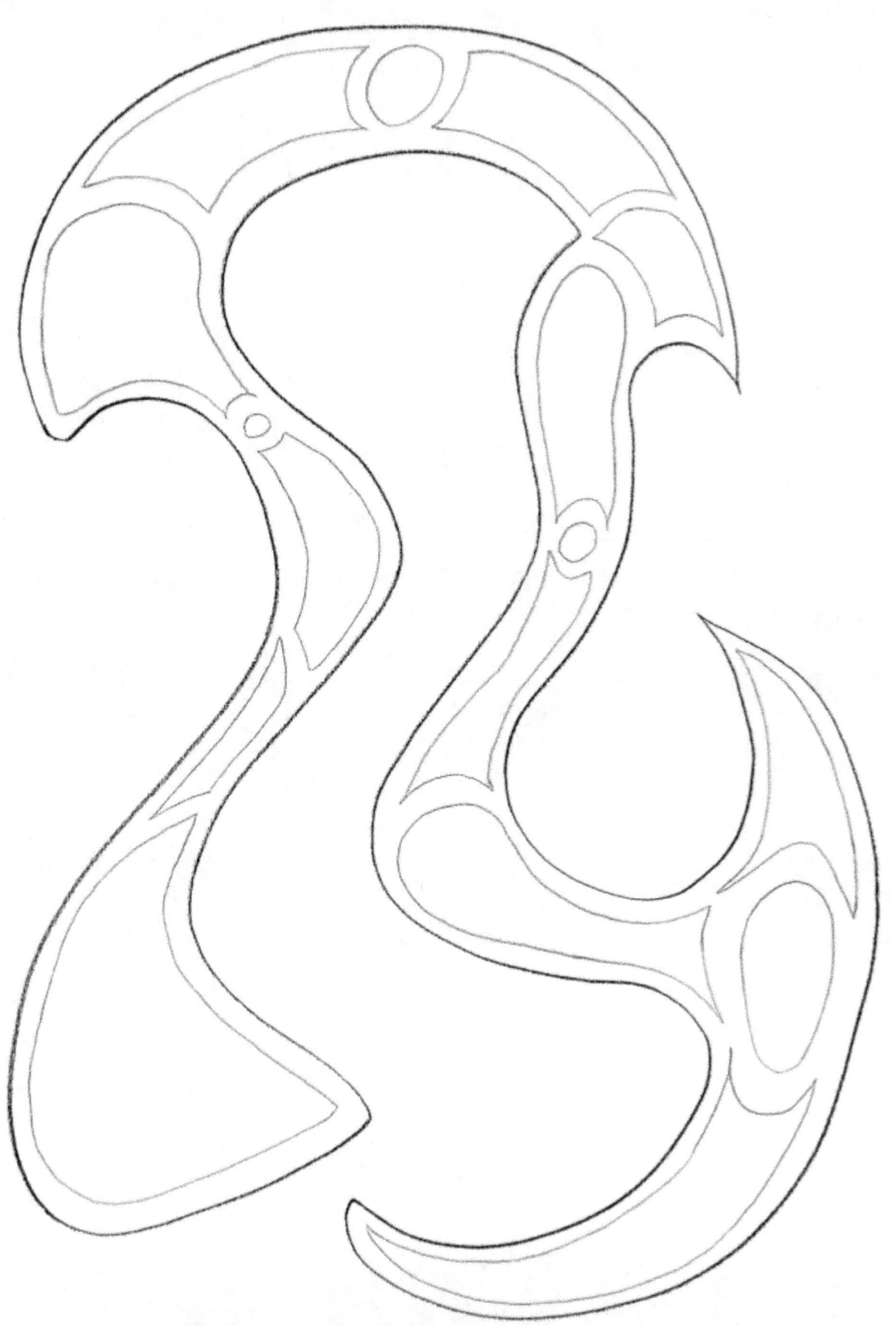

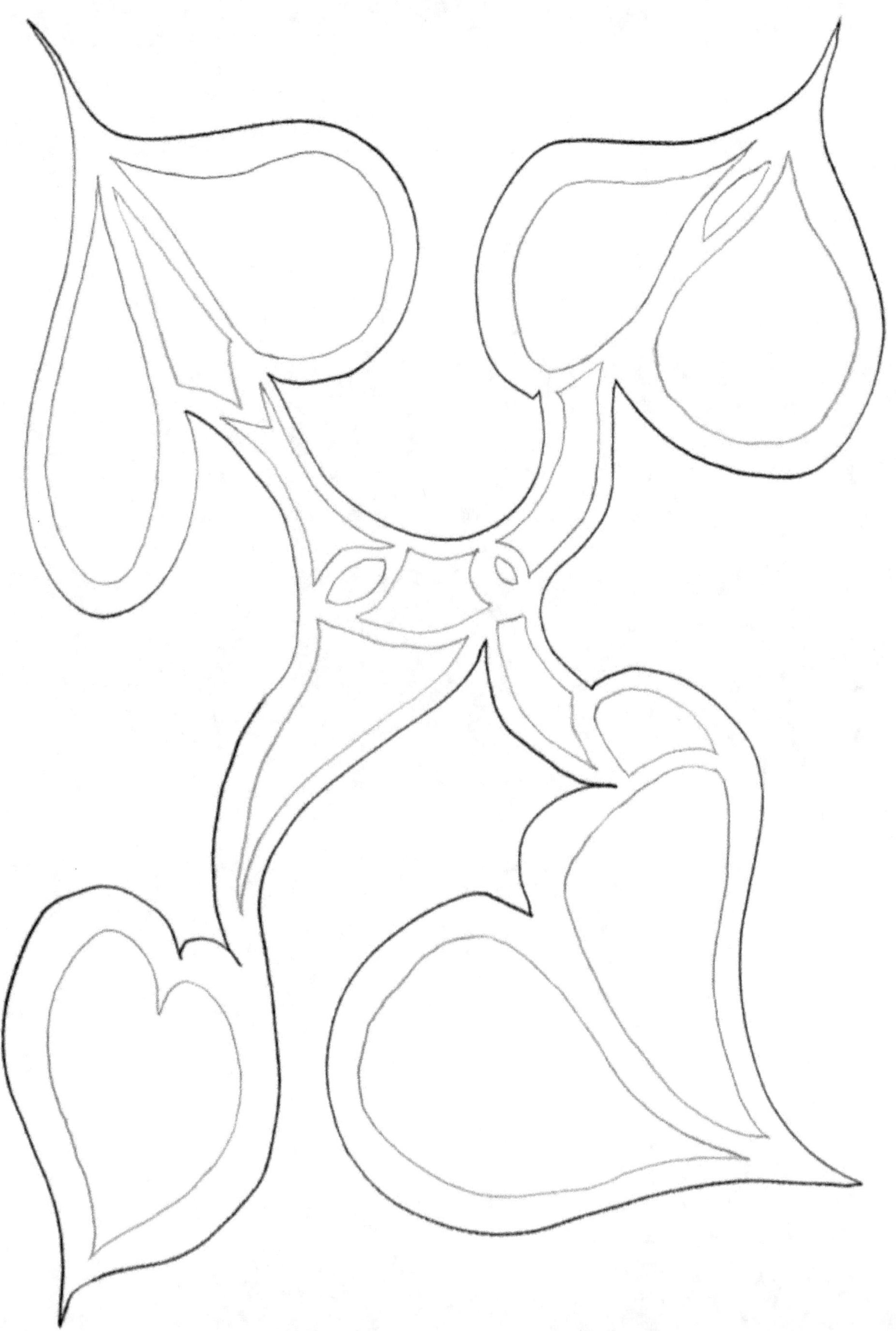

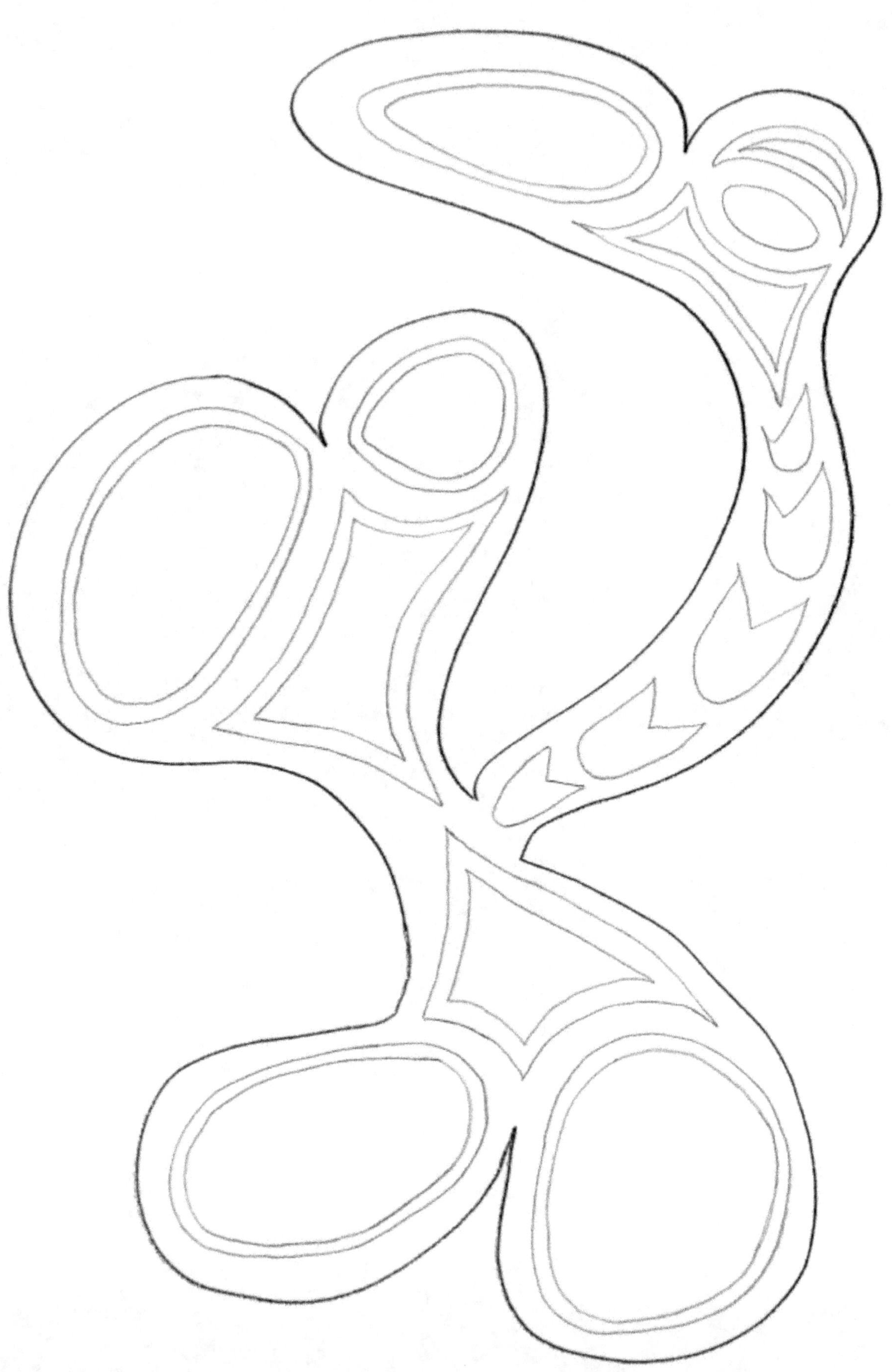

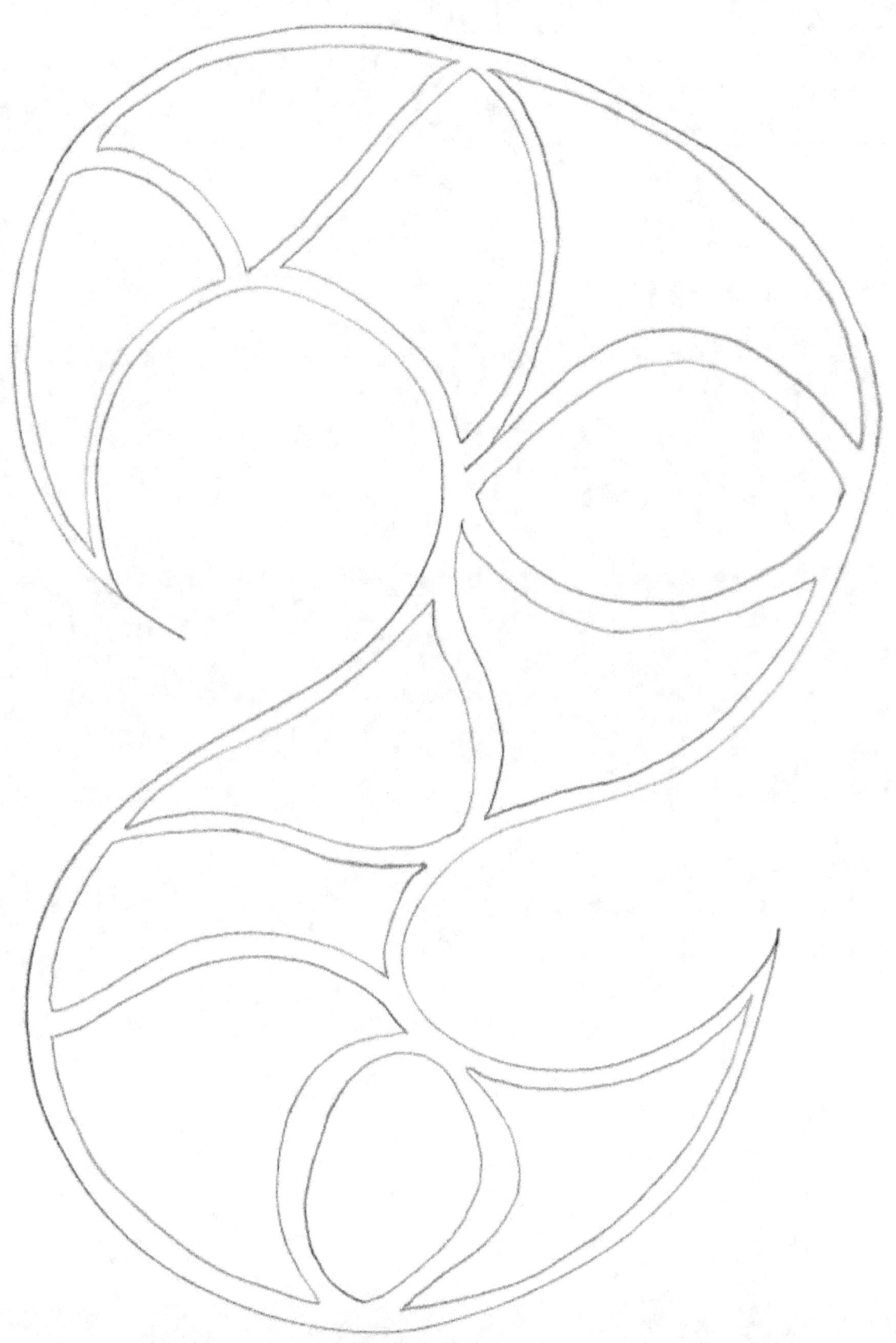

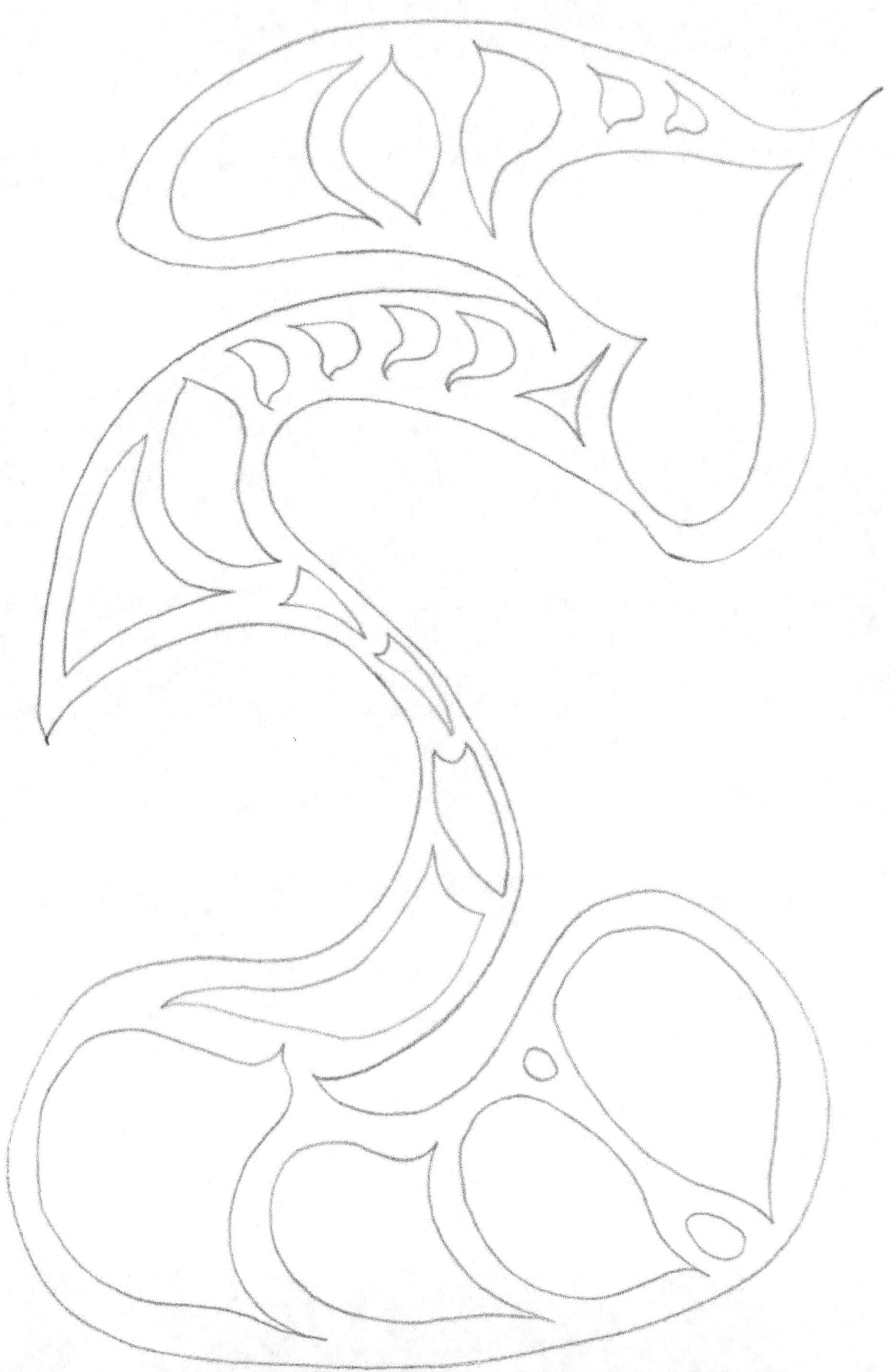

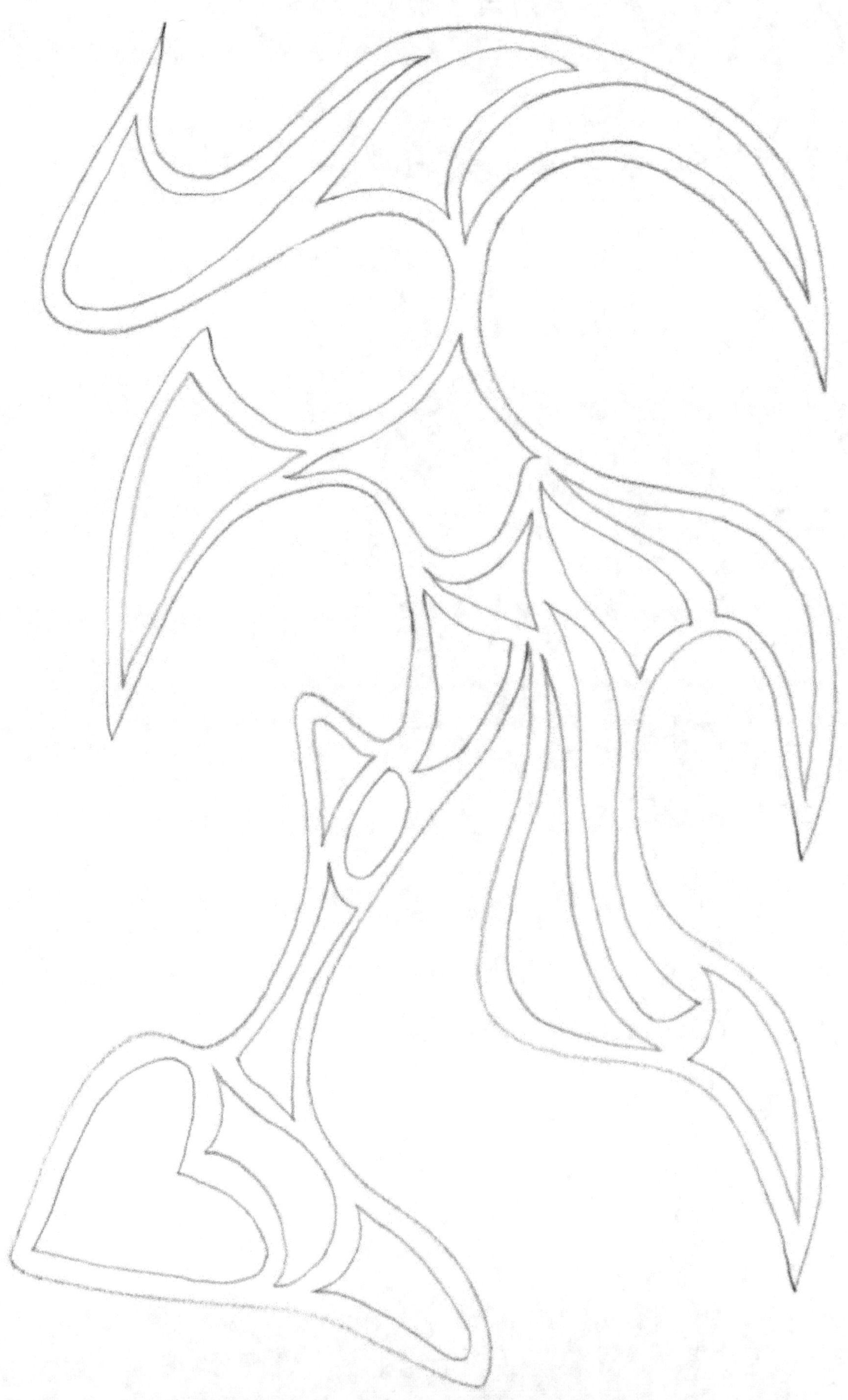

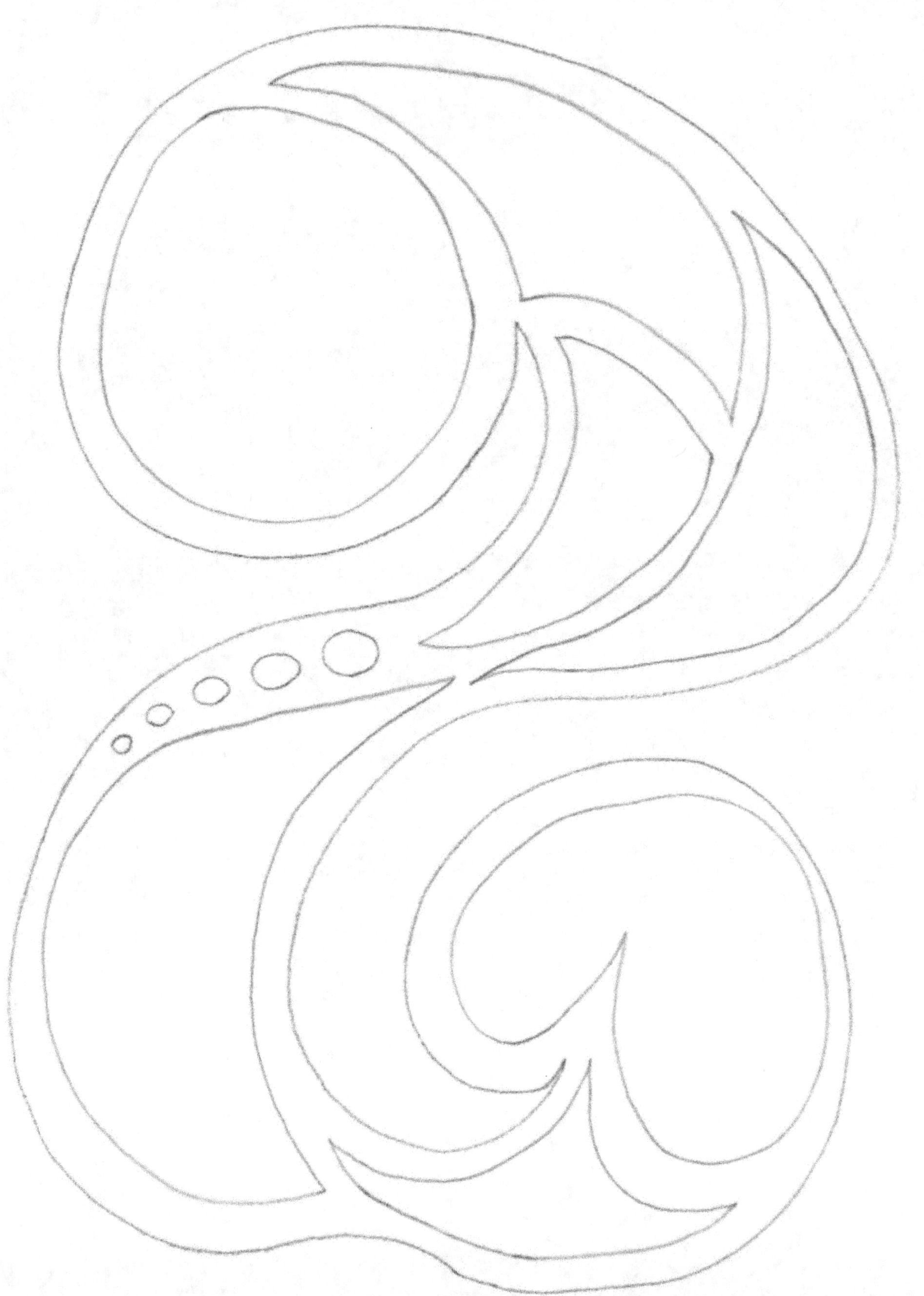

#46Seagulls #ColorMeBrightCB

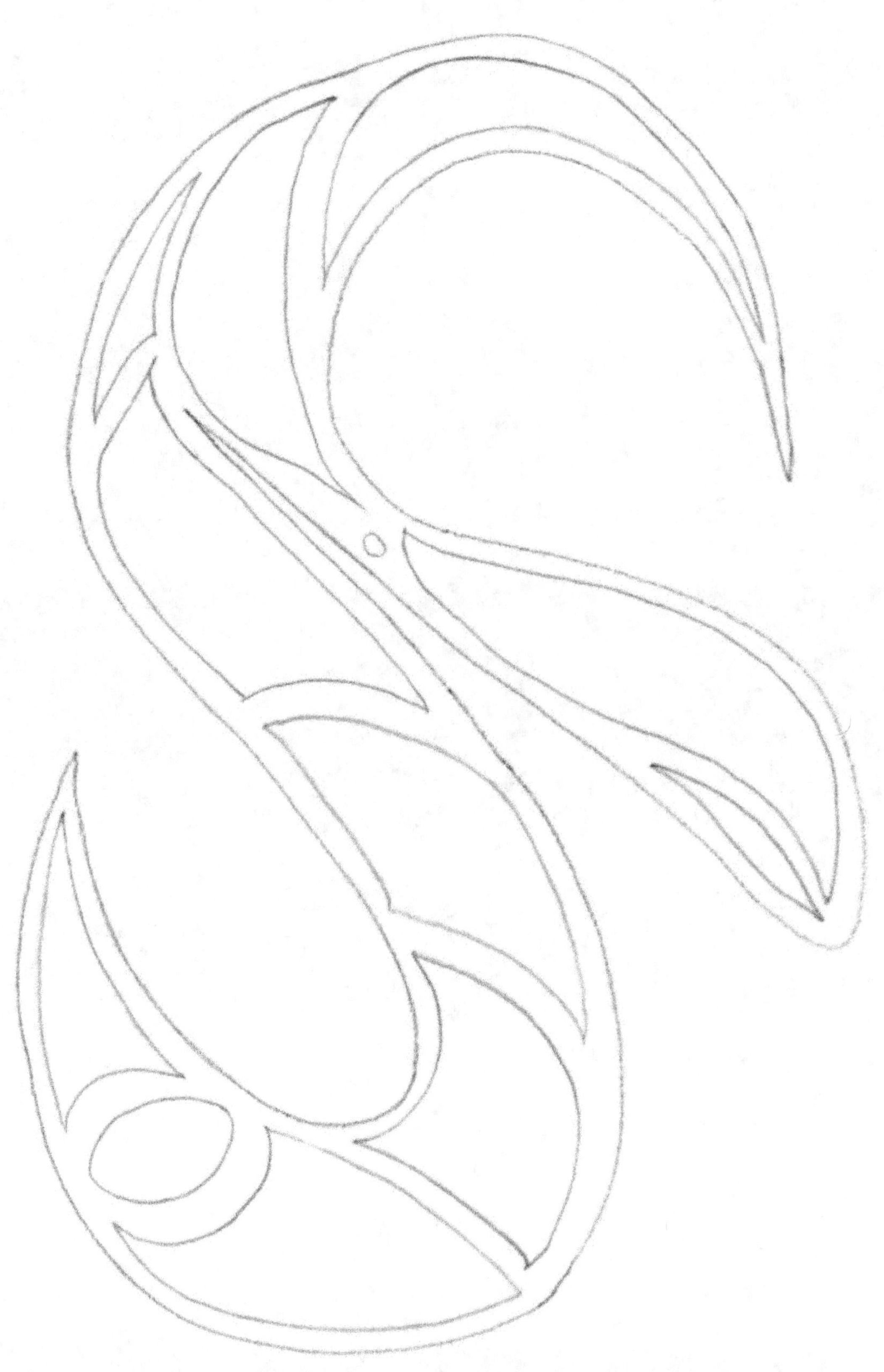

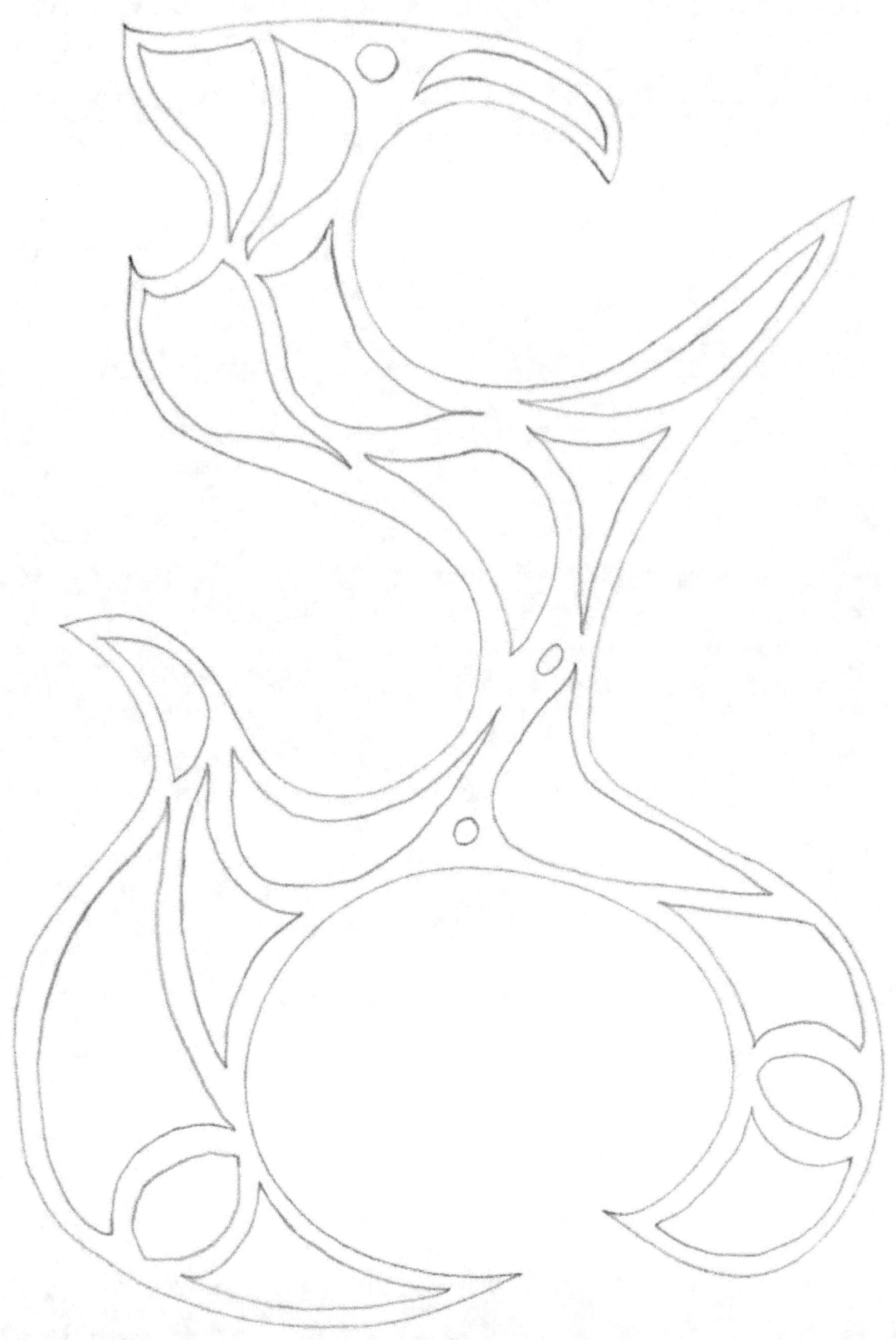

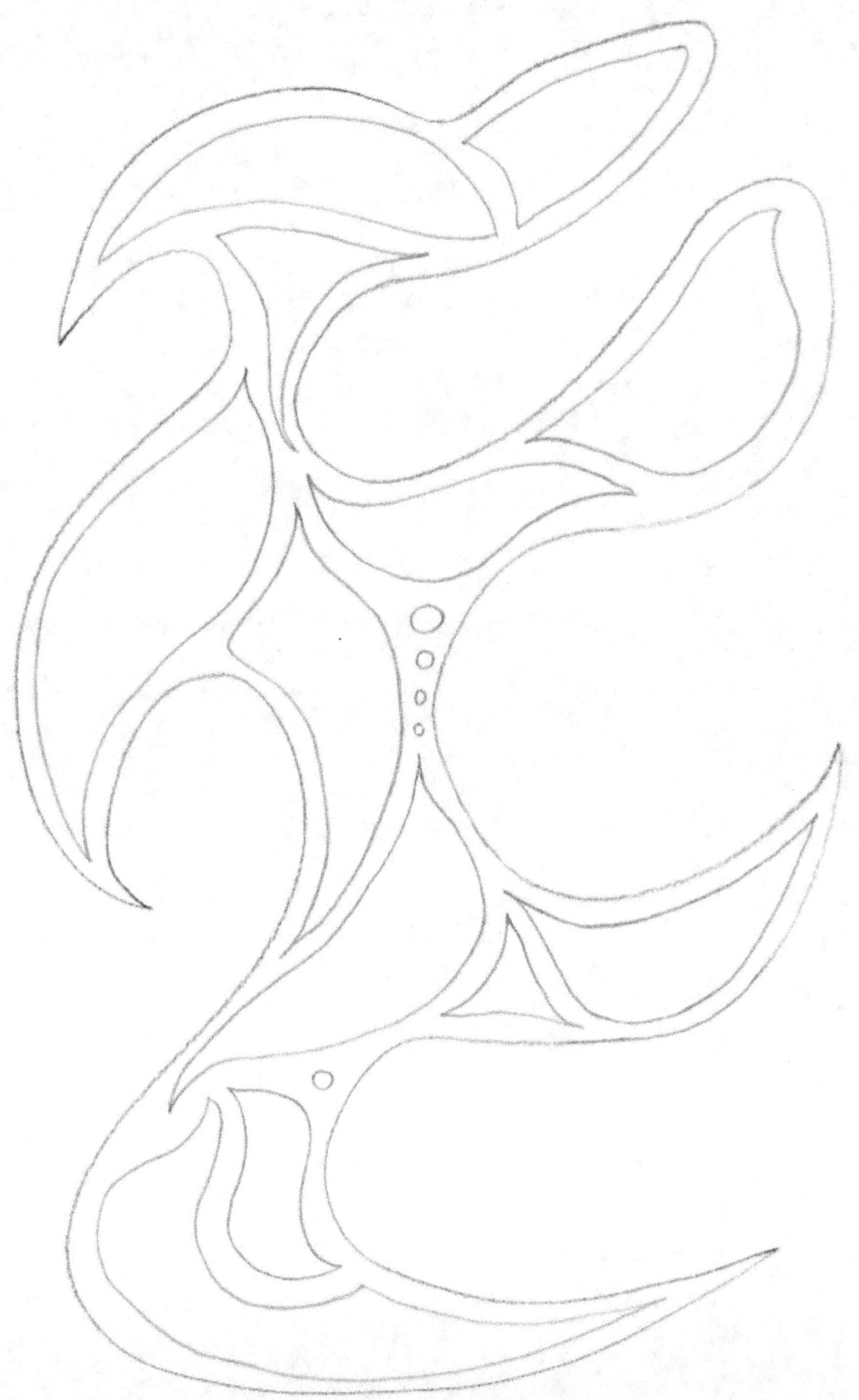

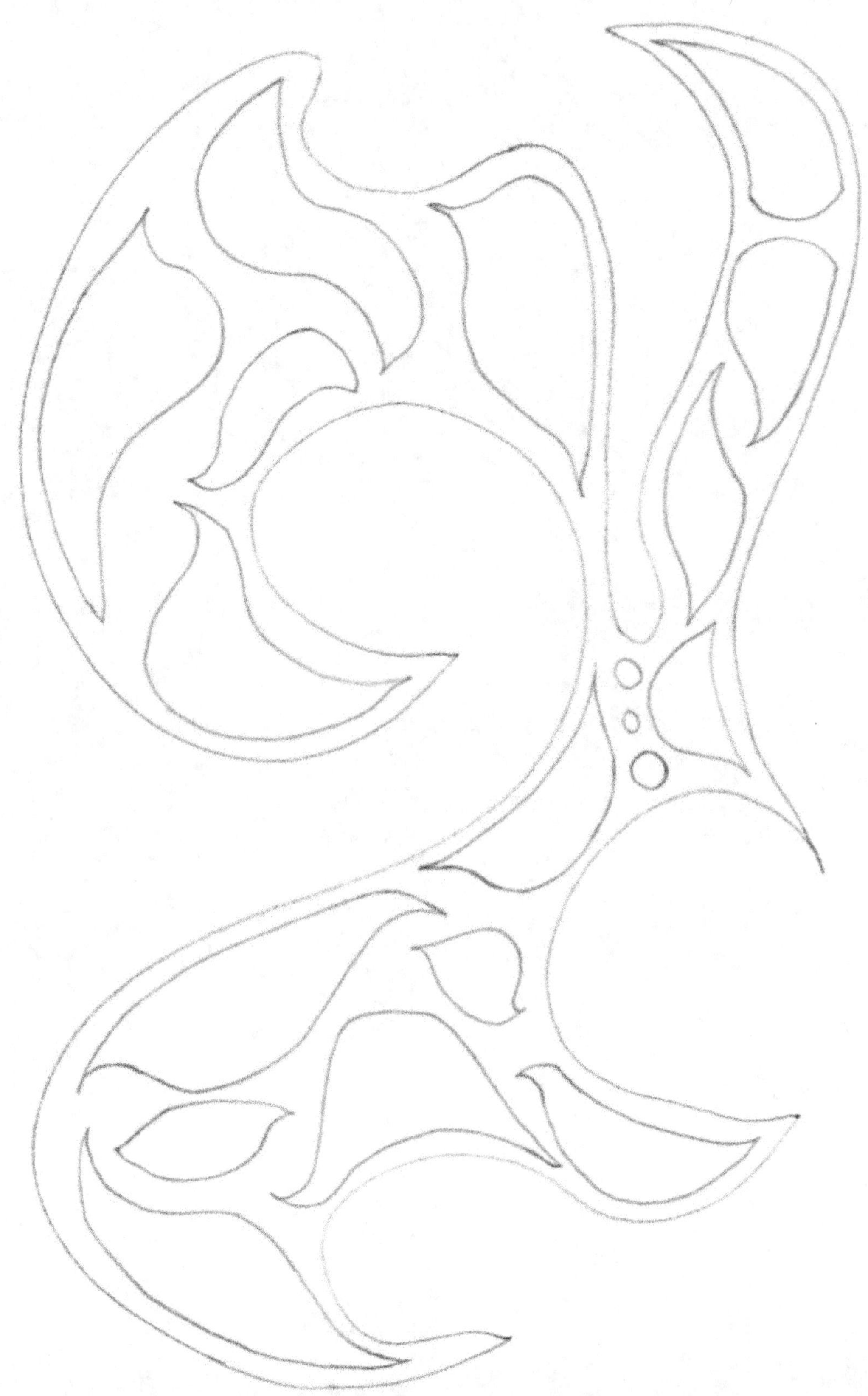

#50Sky #ColorMeBrightCB

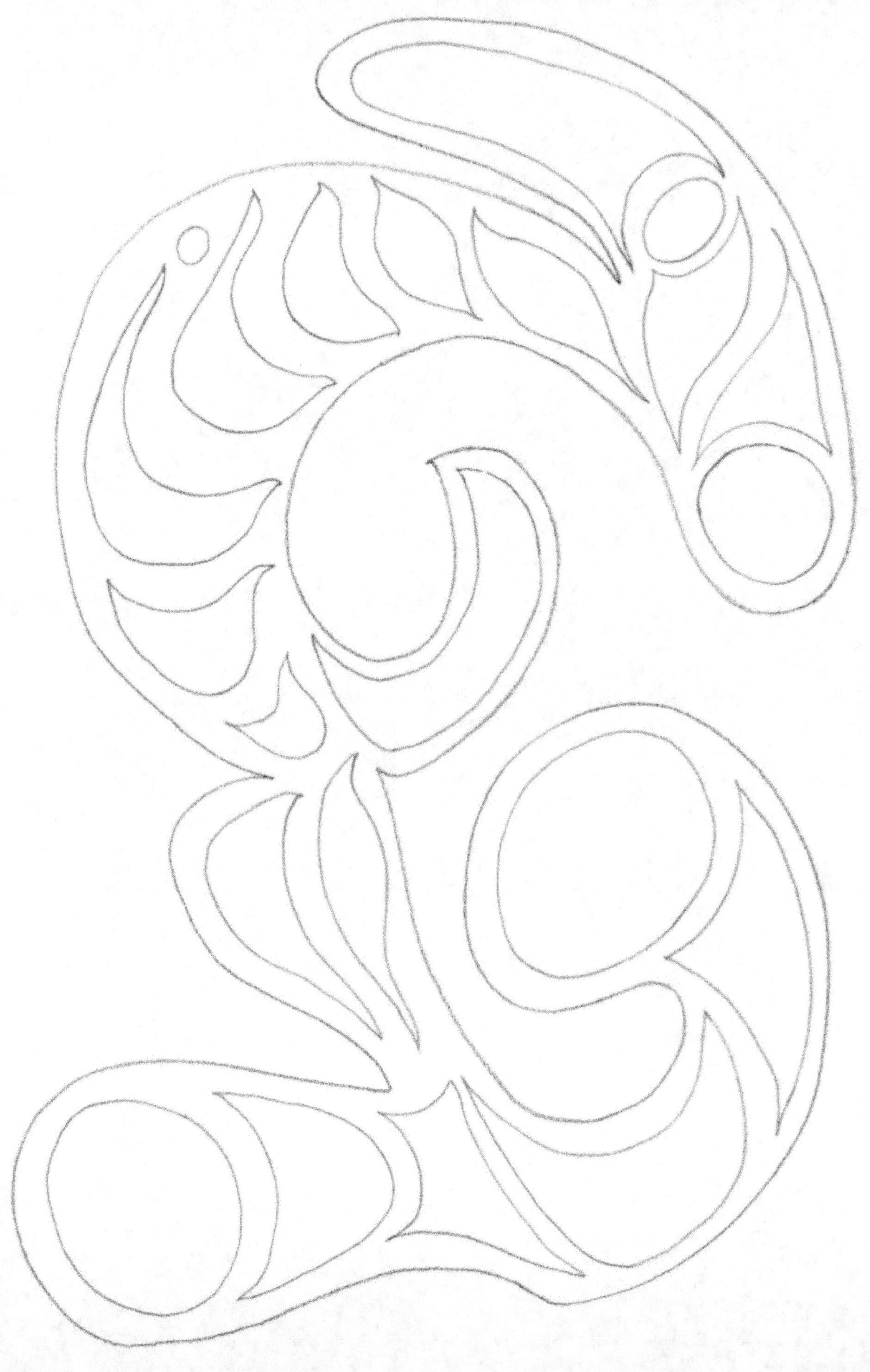

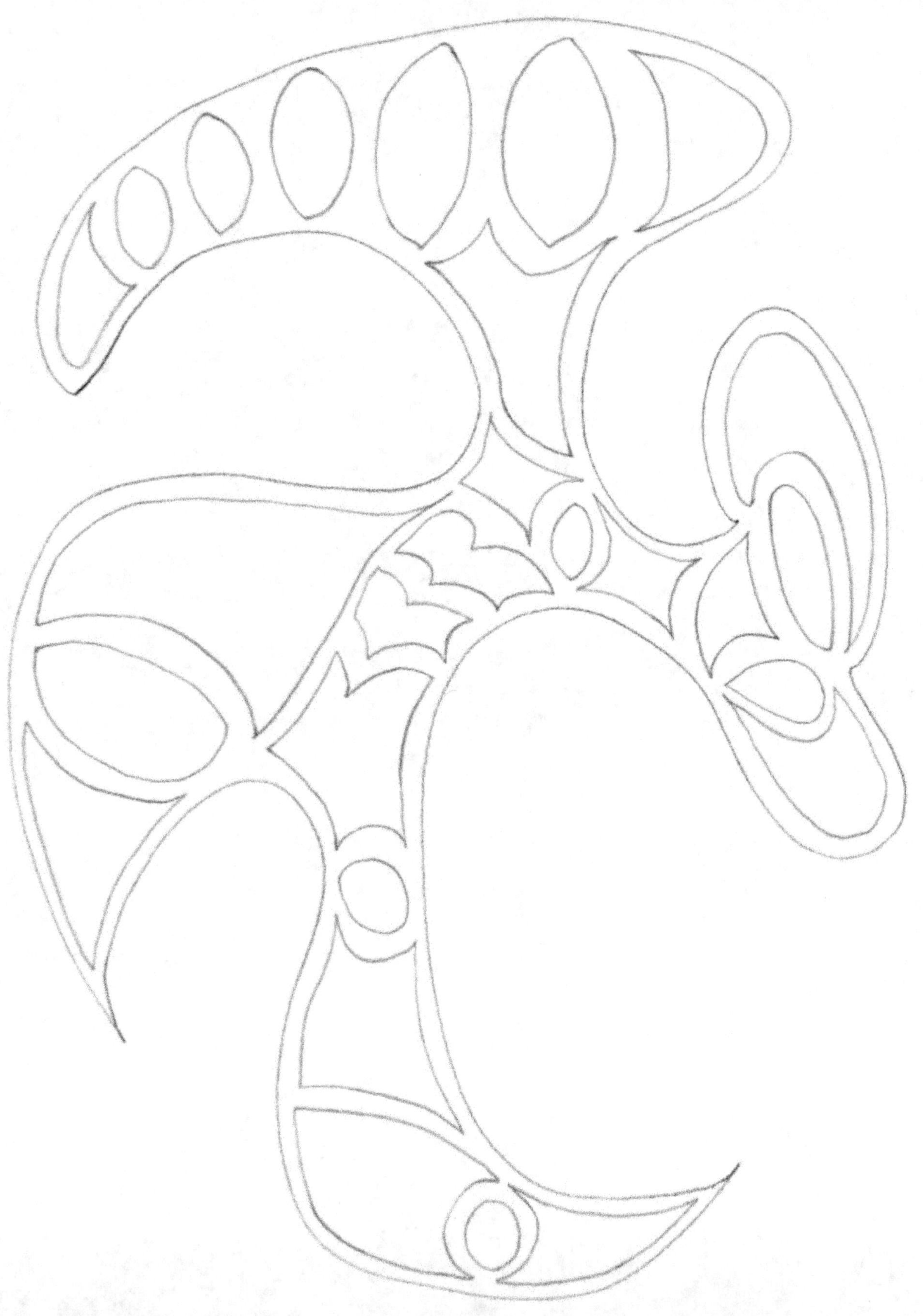

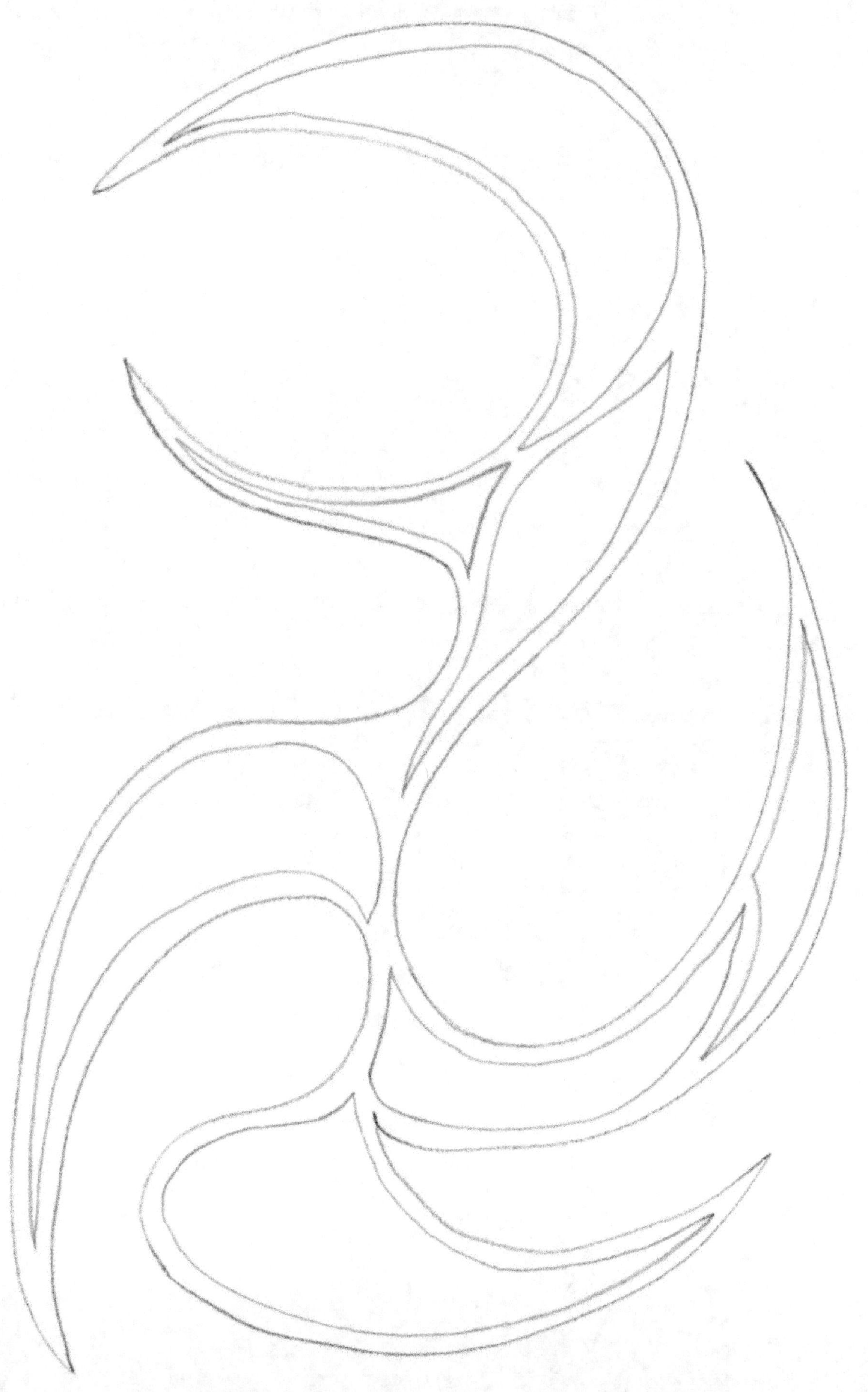

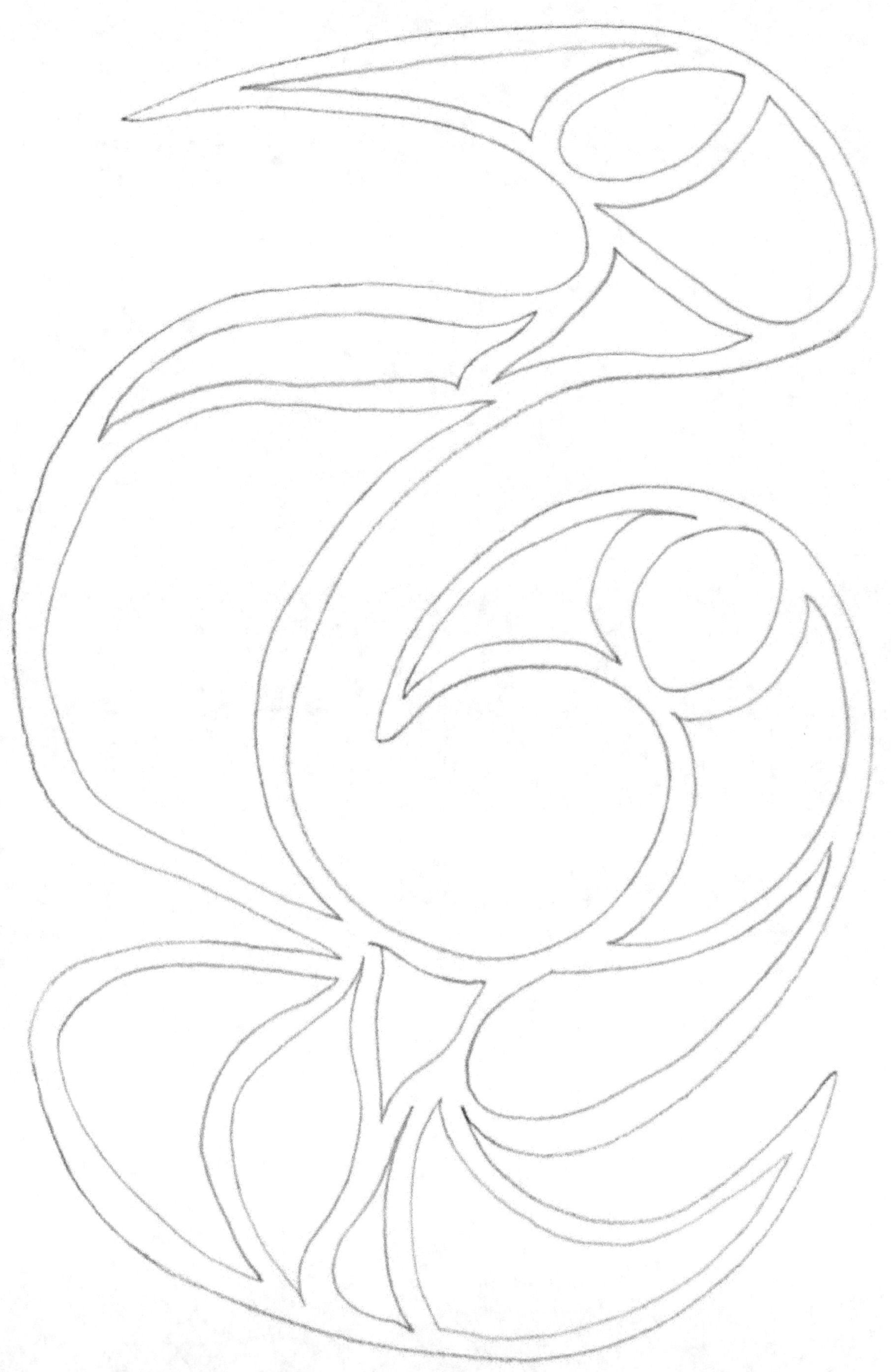

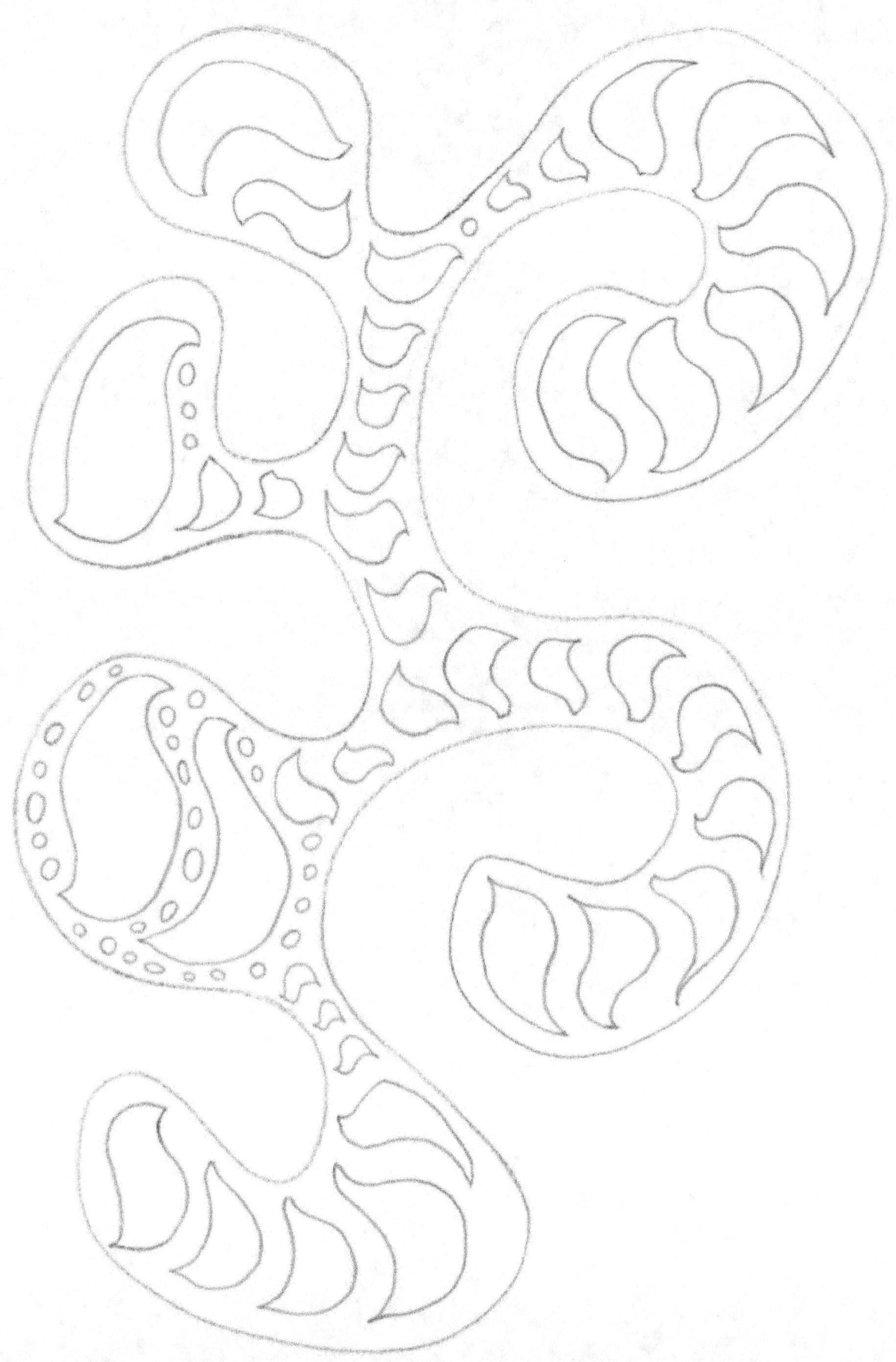

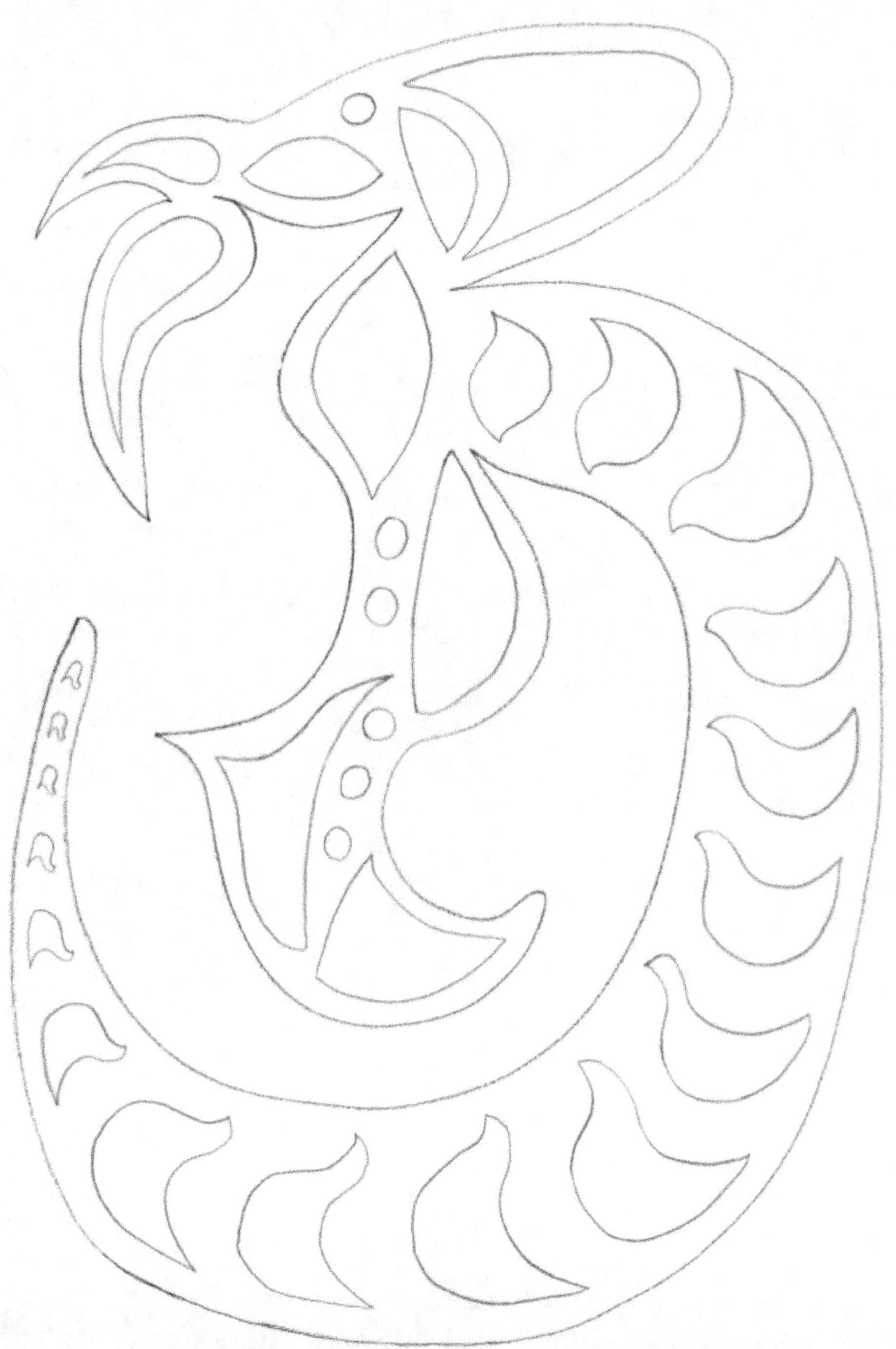

#56Sunsets #ColorMeBrightCB

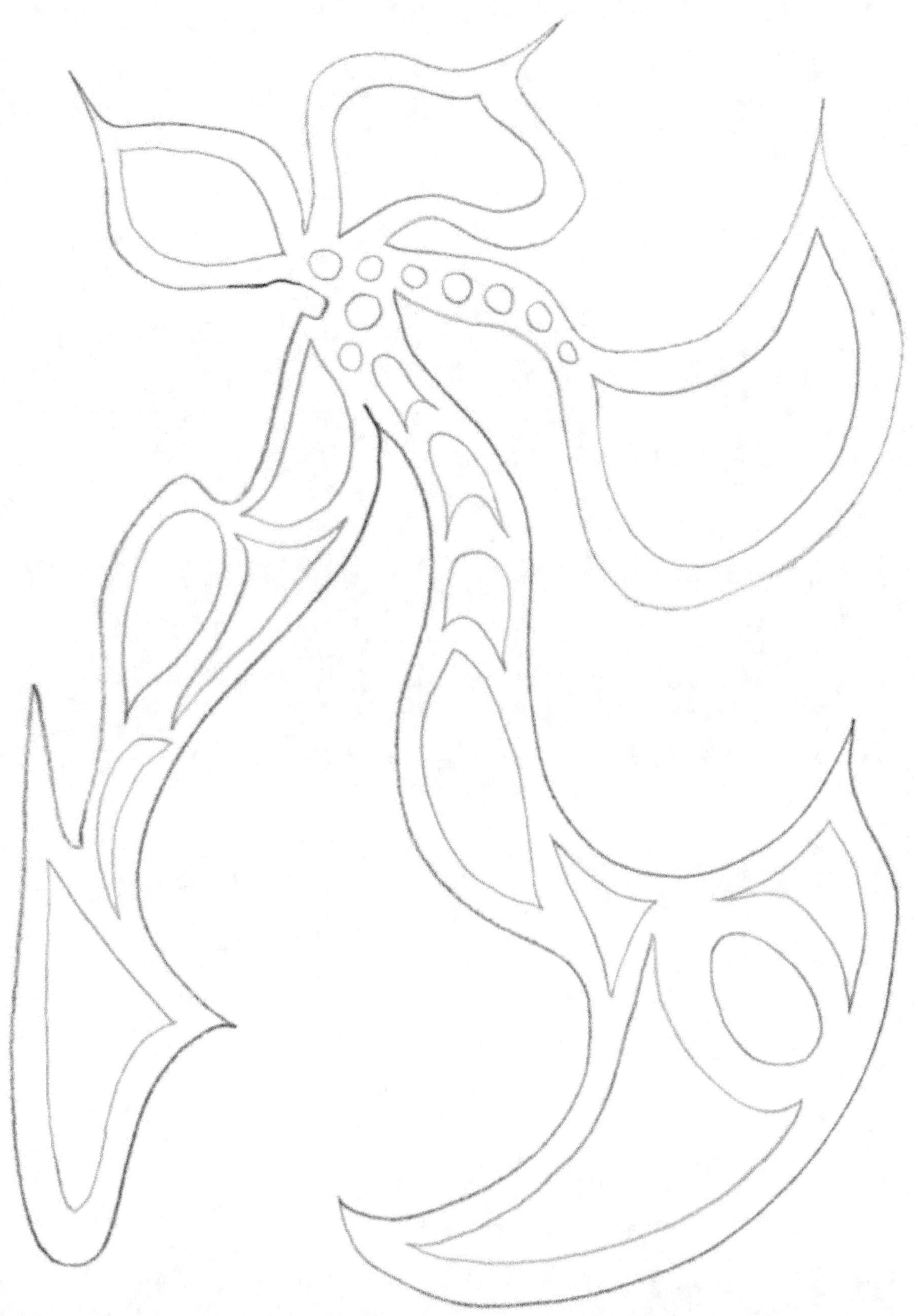

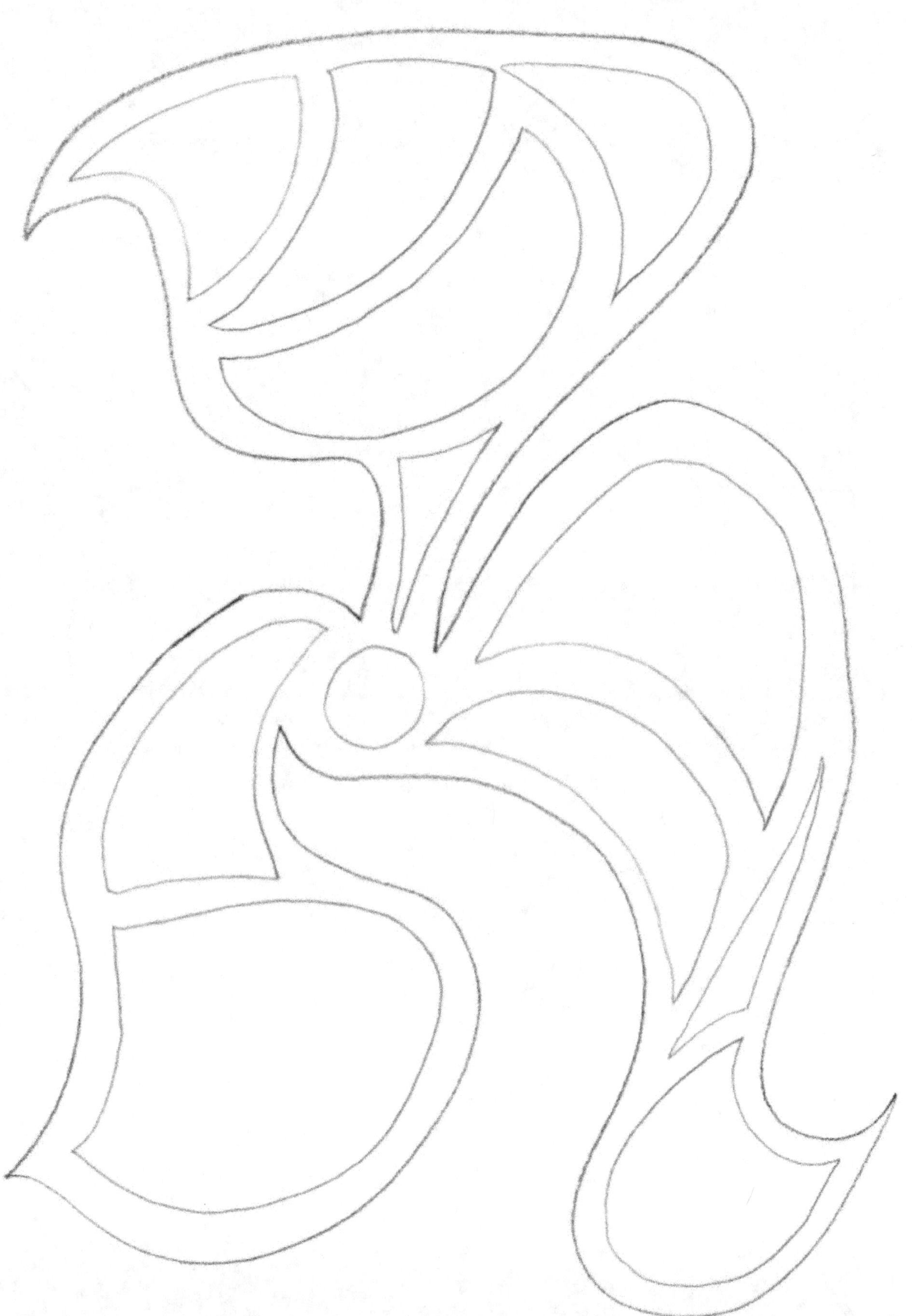

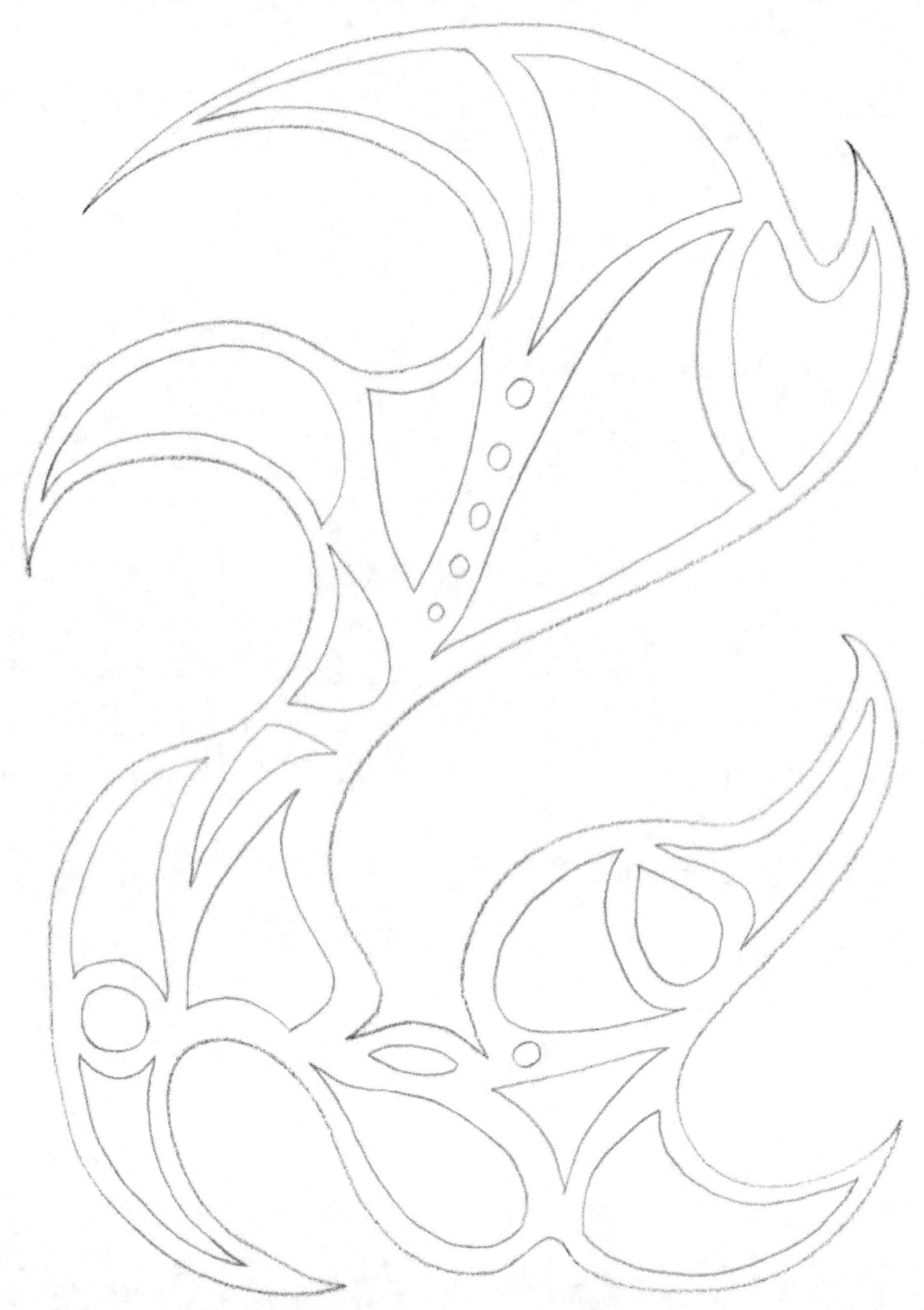

#59Turtles #ColorMeBrightCB

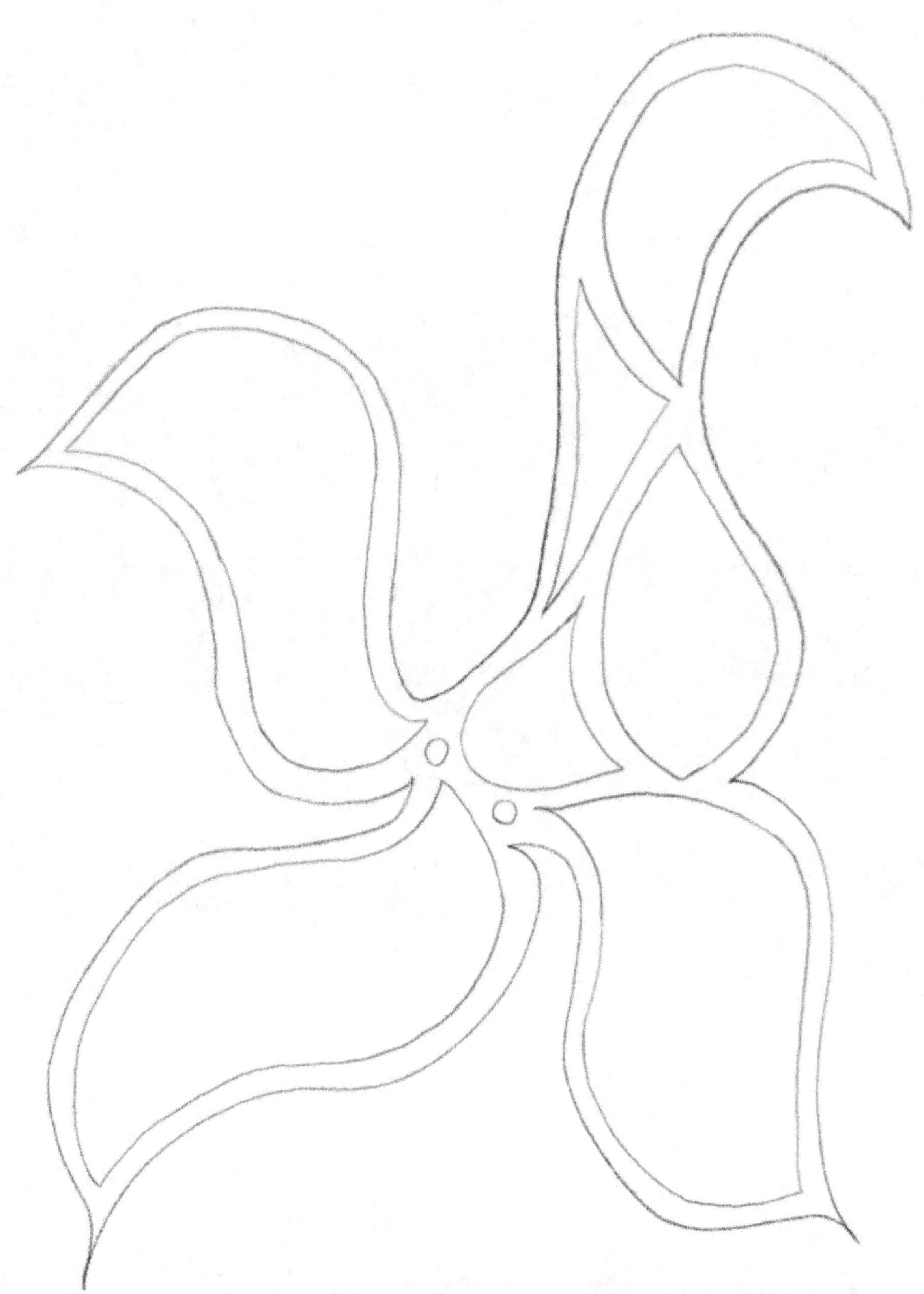

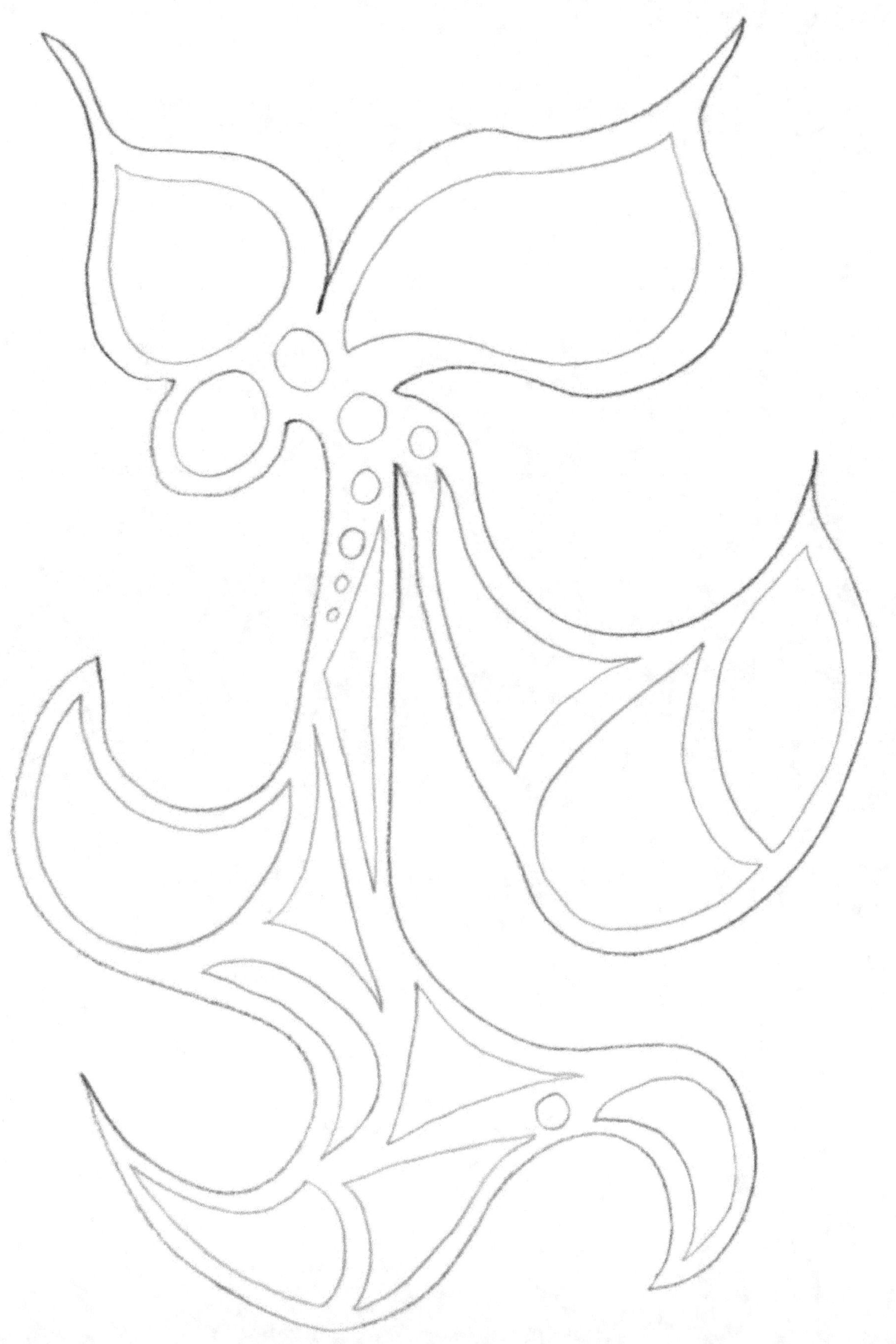

#61Twirl #ColorMeBrightCB

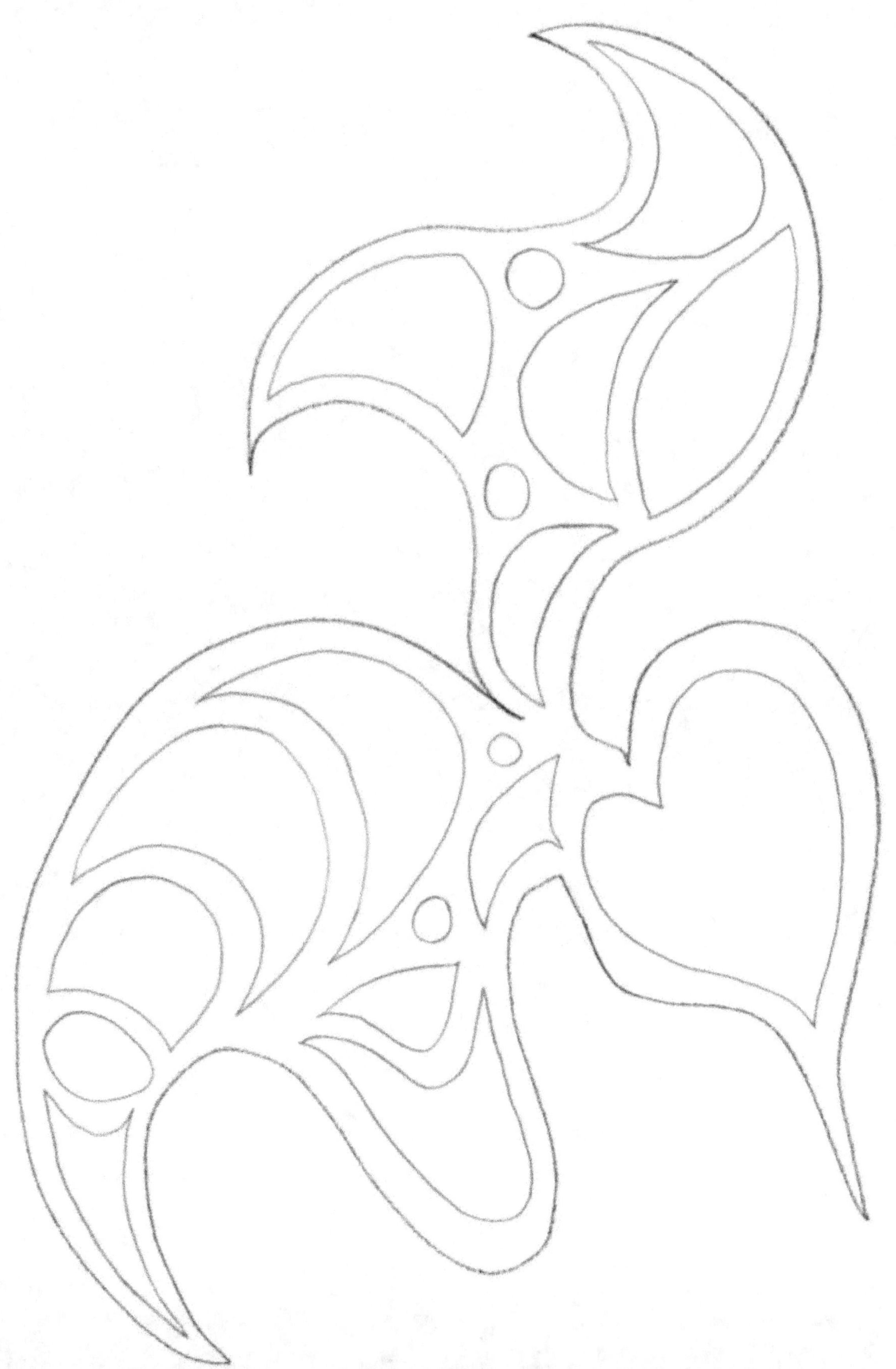

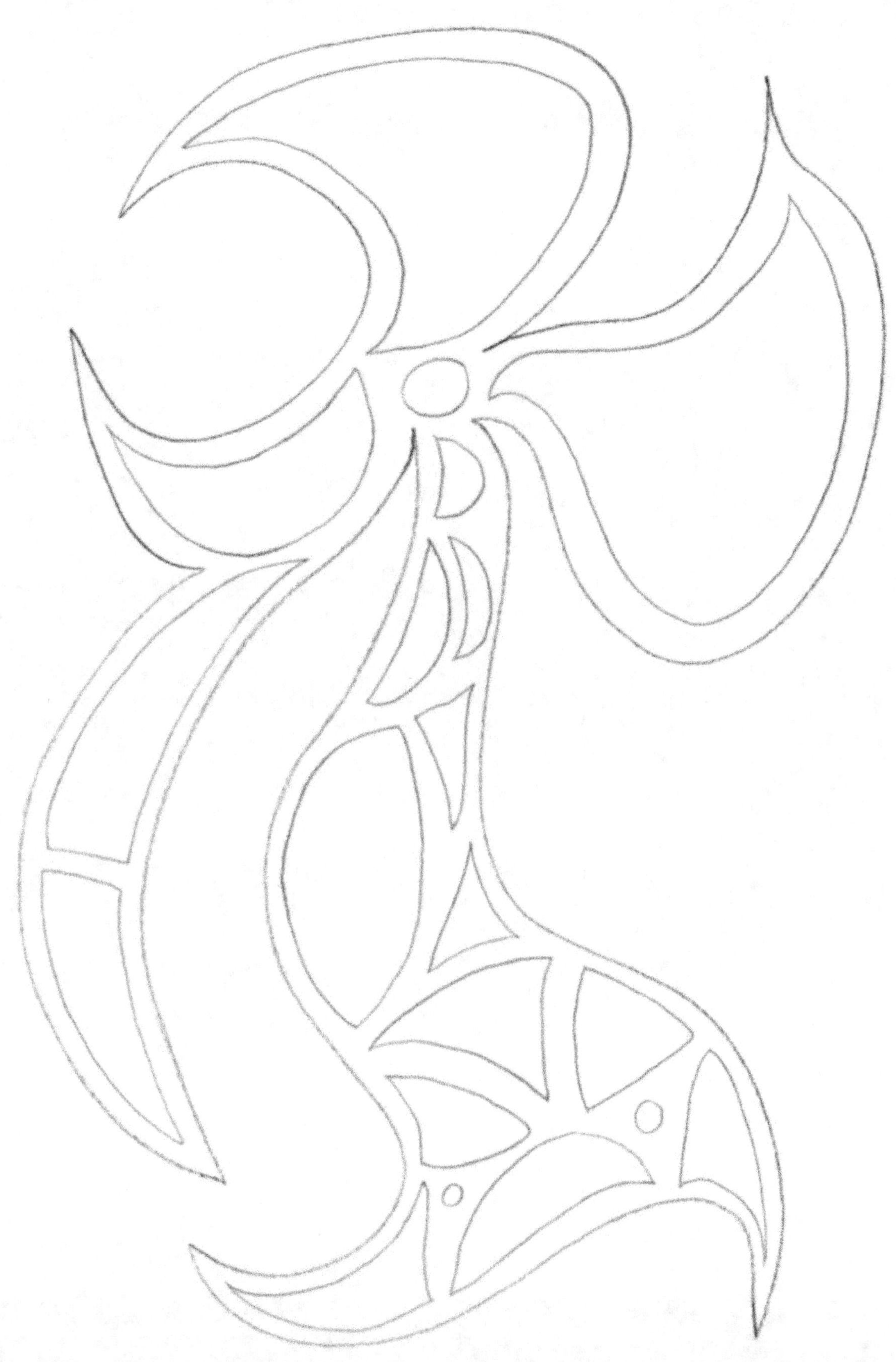

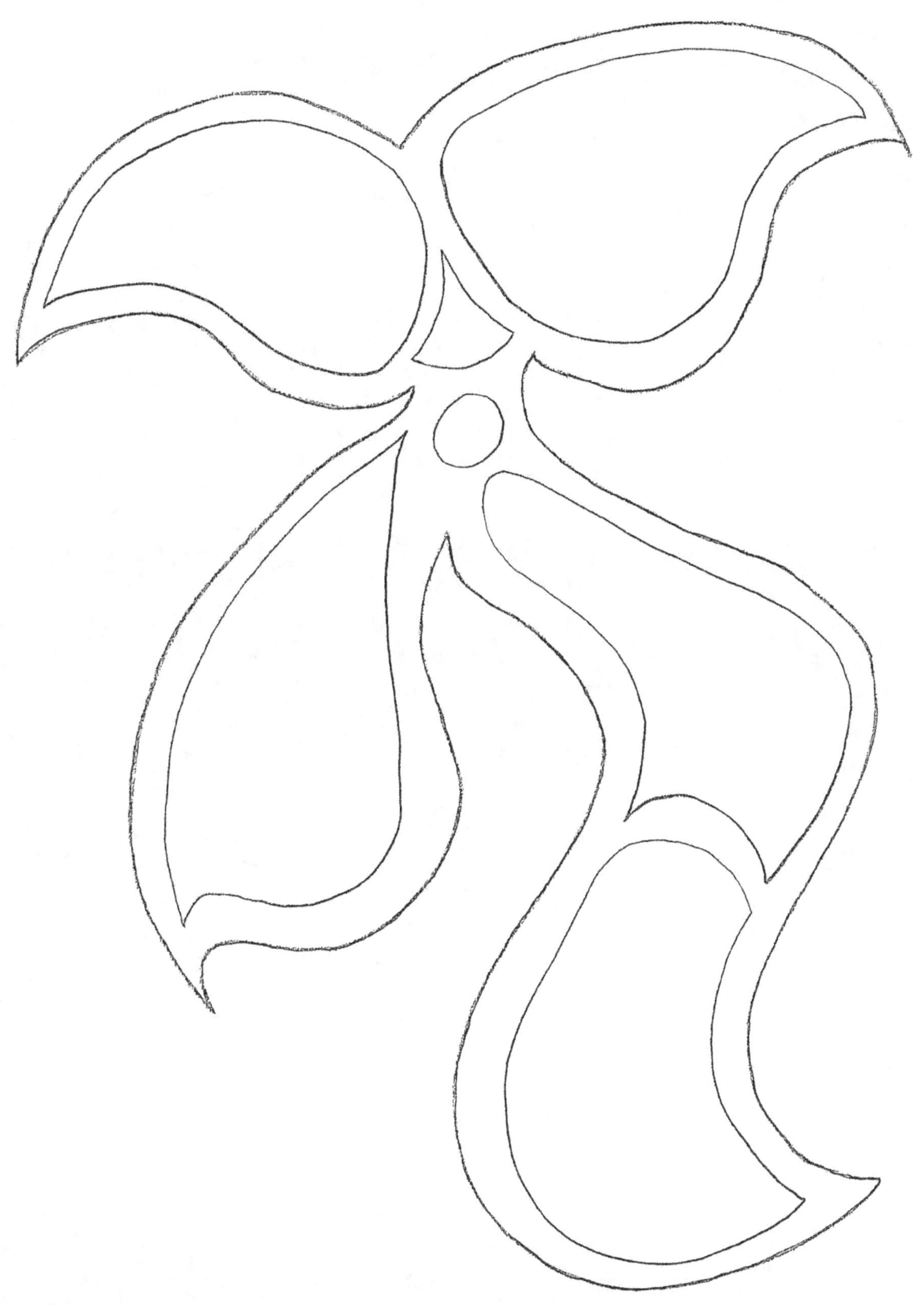

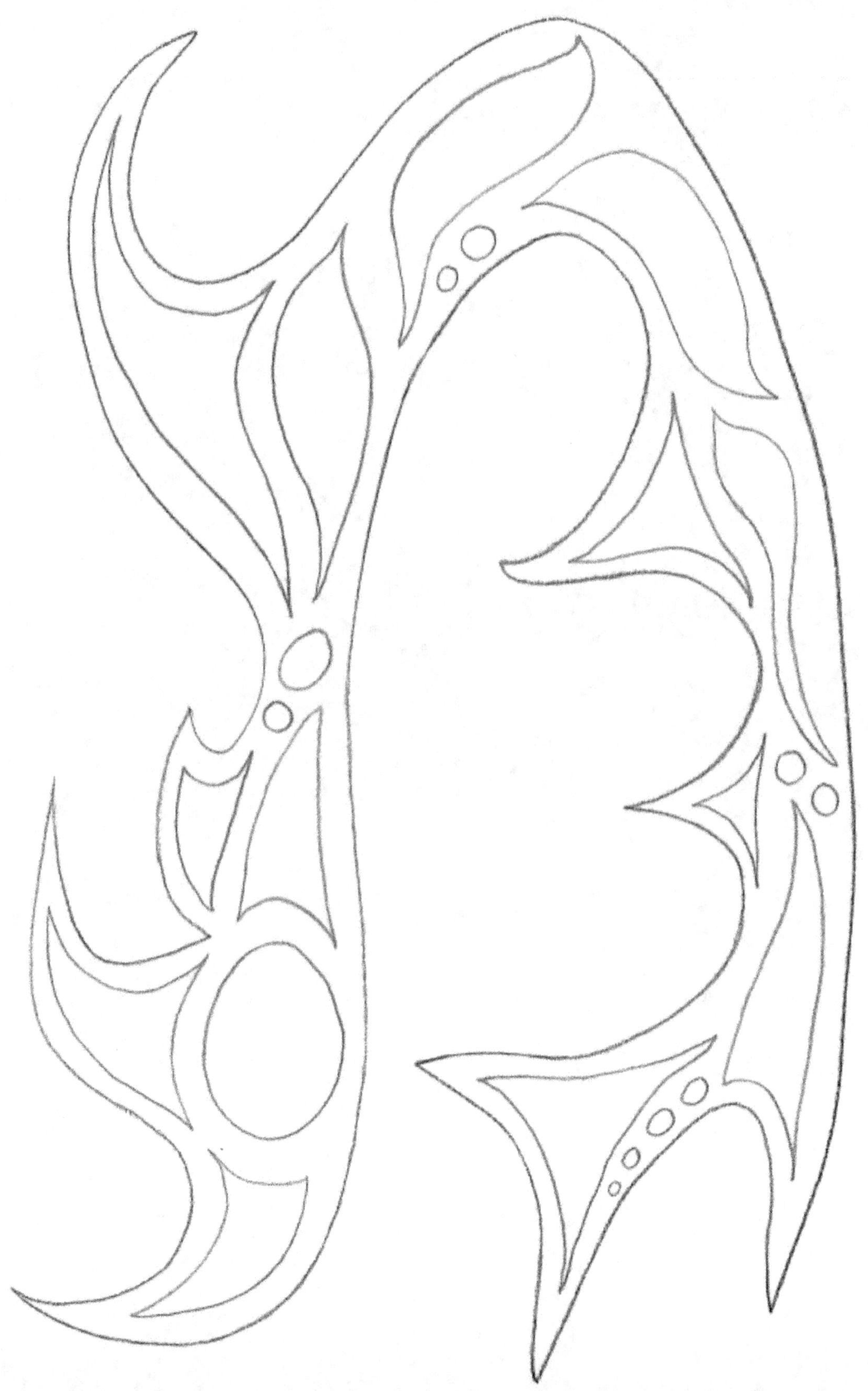

Tester Page

Tester Page

Tester Page

Tester Page

Work by Nadja

Soft-cover books, ebooks, MP3s, and CDs
Smashwords, Amazon, Kindle, CreateSpace, CD Baby, iTunes, YouTube,
and your local bookstore by request

River of Living Light

Evolution Revolution

Random Thoughts and Poems

Hopi Blue Corn

El Maiz Azul de los Hopis

Visionary Tales for the New Earth

Color Me Bright Coloring Book #1

Color Me Bright Coloring Book #1a

Color Me Bright Coloring Book #2

Color Me Bright Coloring Book #2a

Blue Sky

Ascension Codes

Raps, Chants, and Rants

Women's Power Awakened

Ozzengoggle Poems

From the City of Shem

You Are Not Alone

Family Secrets

Flying Heart

Bullies

www.ingramcontent.com/pod-product-compliance
Lightning Source LLC
LaVergne TN
LVHW080321110826
845155LV00026B/174
* 9 7 8 1 9 4 2 0 5 7 9 8 7 *